CONTENTS

HOW TO USE THIS PRICE GUIDE

THE PURPOSE

The second edition of this price guide has been expanded to cover the complete range of children's figures issued by Royal Doulton and Beswick. In the process we have taken liberties with the name of this catalogue, for all figures listed are certainly not derived from storybook characters. However, the great majority are, and thus we have carried the name forward.

As with the other catalogues in Charlton's Royal Doulton reference and pricing library, this publication has been designed to serve two specific purposes. First, to furnish the collector with accurate and detailed listings that provide the essential information needed to build a rewarding collection. Second, to provide collectors and dealers with current market prices for the complete line of Doulton and Beswick storybook figures.

STYLES AND VERSIONS

STYLES: A change in style occurs when a major element of the design is altered or modified as a result of a deliberate mould change. An example of this is *The Duchess With Flowers* (style one) and *The Duchess With a Pie* (style two).

VERSIONS: Versions are modifications in a minor style element, such as the long ears becoming short ears on *Mr. Benjamin Bunny* and *Mr. Jeremy Fisher*'s change in colourways from striped to spotted leggings.

Colourway variations are "version" changes, as no major design element of the mould has been modified.

THE LISTINGS

The Beatrix Potter figures are arranged alphabetically. At the beginning of the Beatrix Potter listings are three pages graphically outlining backstamp variations. Backstamps are illustrated for eight different varieties covering over fifty years of production. In the Beatrix Potter pricing charts, the reader will see Beswick and Doulton model numbers, backstamp numbers and market prices.

The Brambly Hedge figures are listed by their DBH numbers. There are no backstamp variations known.

The Bunnykins figures are arranged in numerical order by DB numbers, with the exception of the first six, which were issued in the late 1930s. These are *Billy, Farmer, Freddie, Mary, Mother* and *Reggie*, and they are arranged alphabetically. There are seven different backstamps to the Bunnykins figures. Please see the section on backstamp variations at the beginning of the Bunnykins listings.

The Snowman series is listed in numerical order by the DS numbers. There are no backstamp variations.

All of the above listings include the modeller, where known, the name of the animal figure, designer, height, colour, date of issue, varieties and series.

A WORD ON PRICING

The purpose of this catalogue is to give readers the most accurate, up-to-date retail prices for storybook figures in the United States, Canada, the United Kingdom and Australia.

To accomplish this, The Charlton Press continues to access an international pricing panel of experts who submit prices based on both dealer and collector retail-price activity, as well as current auction results in the U. S., Canada, the U. K. and Australia for the Bunnykins markets. These market prices are carefully averaged to reflect accurate valuations for figures in each of these markets. All discontinued figures are priced in this manner.

Current figures are priced according to the manufacturer's suggested retail price in each of the four market regions. Please be aware that price or promotional sales discounting is always possible and can result in lower prices than those listed.

The prices published herein are for figures in mint condition. Collectors are cautioned that a repaired or restored piece may be worth as little as 50 percent of the value of the same figure in mint condition.

A further word on pricing. As mentioned previously, this is a catalogue giving prices for figures in the currency of a particular market (U.S. dollars for the American market and sterling for the U.K. market). The bulk of the prices given herein are not determined by currency exchange calculations, but by actual market activity in the market concerned.

One exception, however, occurs in the case of current figures or recent limited editions issued in only one of the four markets. Since such items were priced by Doulton only in the country in which they were to be sold, prices for the other markets have been calculated using current currency exchange rates. These prices are noted with an asterisk.

Additionally, collectors must remember that all relevant information must be known to make a proper valuation of price. When comparing auction prices to catalogue prices, collectors and dealers must remember two important points. First, compare "apples and apples." Be sure that auction prices realized for figures include a buyer's premium if one is due. Buyer's premiums can range from 10 to 15 percent, and on an expensive piece this amount can be substantial. Secondly, know whether a figure is restored, repaired or in mint condition. This fact may not be noted or explained in the listings, and as a result, its price will not be reflective of that same piece in mint condition. Please be aware of repairs and restorations and the effect they may have on values.

A last word of caution. No pricing catalogue can be, or should be, a fixed price list. This catalogue must be considered a pricing guide only—showing the most current retail prices based on market demand within a particular region for the various figures.

INTRODUCTION
By Louise Irvine

THE HISTORY OF STORYBOOK CHARACTERS FROM THE ROYAL DOULTON, JOHN BESWICK AND ROYAL ALBERT STUDIOS

For over a century, the Royal Doulton Studios have entertained us with storybook characters, particularly animals endowed with human personalities. In Victorian times, a group of frogs enacting a well-known fable raised a smile in much the same way as the antics of the BRAMBLY HEDGE™ mice amuse us today. The tales of BEATRIX POTTER™, with lots of different animals acting and conversing as if they were human, are as popular now as when they were first written in the early 1900s. Similarly the BUNNYKINS™ characters, first created in the 1930s, have survived the vagaries of fashion to become the most popular collectables of the 1990s. Obviously the idea of a creature simultaneously human and animal is deep rooted in our literary culture, and it is interesting to trace when it first became apparent in the Doulton world.

A Tinworth mouse group

The Doulton factory was founded in London in 1815, but for the first 50 years production was confined to practical pottery. In the late 1860s, Sir Henry Doulton established an art studio, employing students from the Lambeth School of Art to decorate vases, jugs and plaques in fashionable Victorian styles. Some artists specialised in figurative sculpture, notably George Tinworth, who was the first to seek inspiration from well-known stories. The Bible provided him with most of his subject matter, but he also enjoyed reading the fables of Aesop and La Fontaine. These moralistic tales feature foxes, mice, lions and other creatures exemplifying human traits, and they fascinated the Victorians, particularly after the publication of Darwin's theory of evolution. Tinworth modelled several fables groups in the 1880s, including *The Fox and the Ape*, *The Cat and the Cheese* and *The Ox and the Frogs.* Later he produced mice and frog subjects, based on his own observations of human nature, which reflect his perceptive sense of humour.

The potential for dressed-up animals to disguise a deeper message soon led to their widespread use in children's literature, notably *Alice's Adventures in Wonderland* and Lear's nonsense poems. In 1908, Kenneth Grahame wrote *Wind in the Willows* to comment on the behaviour of the English aristocracy, but the exciting adventures of Mr. Toad subtly conceal the author's critical stance. The dapper toad in his pinstripes and tails was modelled shortly afterwards by Lambeth artist Francis Pope, and a companion piece shows Mr. Toad disguised as a washerwoman in order to escape from prison.

Figures like these probably encouraged Beatrix Potter to approach the Lambeth studio in 1908 with a view to having her own animal characters immortalised in ceramic. Miss Potter published several illustrated stories about her favourite animals after the success of *The Tale*

Mr. Toad disguised as a washerwoman

of Peter Rabbit™ in 1902, and some characters had already appeared as cuddly toys and decorative motifs on clothes, etc. Unfortunately an earlier contract with a German china firm made any arrangement with Doulton impossible, but she tried on a later occasion to have figures made of her characters at Grimwade's factory in Stoke-on-Trent. They suggested that Doulton's other factory in Burslem would be the best place to have the figures decorated, but again plans fell through. It was not until after Miss Potter's death that her dream was realised when the John Beswick factory in Longton began making little figures inspired by her books.

The John Beswick factory was founded in 1894 to produce ornamental jugs, vases and other decorative fancies. By the 1940s the Beswick artists had established a reputation for quality animal modelling, particularly portraits of famous horses by Arthur Gredington. In 1947, Gredington demonstrated his versatility when he modelled *Jemima Puddleduck* at the suggestion of Lucy Beswick, the wife of the managing director. She had been inspired by a visit to Beatrix Potter's Lake District home, where many of the tales are set. The success of this first study led to an initial collection of ten Beatrix Potter characters, including *Peter Rabbit, Benjamin Bunny* and *Mrs. Tiggy Winkle.*

Launched in 1948, the new Beatrix Potter figures were welcomed with enthusiasm, and it was not long before

A group of Beatrix Potter books with the figures beside

Gredington was at work on another collection of character animals, this time from an American animated film. The *Lion* cartoon by David Hand was released in 1948, and Zimmy the Lion became a new star for the Rank Film Organisation. Sequel cartoons introduced Ginger Nutt, Hazel Nutt, Dinkum Platypus, Loopy Hare, Oscar Ostrich, Dusty Mole and Felia Cat, all of which were modelled in 1949 as the *DAVID HAND'S ANIMALAND*™ series. David Hand had formerly worked for the Walt Disney studios, directing *Mickey Mouse* shorts, as well as the major films *Snow White* and *Bambi,* and it was not long before these cartoons also inspired a collection of Beswick figures. Arthur Gredington modelled the little figures of *Snow White and the Seven Dwarfs* whilst Jan Granoska, a trainee modeller, was given the task of portraying *Mickey Mouse and Friends,* plus some characters from *Pinocchio* and *Peter Pan.*

Although Miss Granoska was only at the Beswick studio for three years, she was responsible for some of their most desirable figures, including the *Monkey Band,* which continued the musical animal theme established by Mr. Gredington's *Cat Orchestra* and still enjoyed today with the new PIG PROMENADE™. Music (of sorts!) is also being played by the BEDTIME CHORUS™, a group of enthusiastic children accompanied by a singing cat and dog. These were amongst the first character figures to be modelled by Albert Hallam, who gradually took over responsibility for this area in the 1960s. As head mouldmaker, Hallam had made many of the production moulds for Gredington designs, so he was already familiar with the subject matter. He continued the *Beatrix Potter* collection, adding characters such as *Old Mr. Brown* and *Cecily Parsley,* and in 1968 he launched a new Disney series based on their newest cartoon hit, *Winnie the Pooh and the Blustery Day.*

The late 1960s was a time of transition for the company, as Ewart Beswick was ready to retire but he had no heir for his successful business. Fortunately the Royal Doulton group was in the midst of an expansion programme and they acquired the Beswick factory in 1969. They soon benefited from Beswick's expertise in the field of character animals, as Albert Hallam began modelling little figures inspired by their famous Bunnykins nurseryware.

The Bunnykins characters were originally created in the 1930s by Barbara Vernon, a young nun who taught

Artist Bunnykins **with the nurseryware plate which inspired the figure**

in an English convent school. She often entertained her pupils with sketches and stories about the Bunnykins characters and their potential as nurseryware decoration was recognised by her father Cuthbert Bailey, who was Doulton's managing director at the time. Bunnykins was launched in 1934 and, sixty years later, it is still one of the world's best-selling nurseryware patterns.

There had been an attempt in 1939 to start a collection of Bunnykins figures, but the Second World War intervened and production was not resumed, making the first six characters very rare indeed. Nine new style figures by Albert Hallam were launched in 1972, followed by three more the following year, and they were all derived from characters in the Bunnykins nurseryware scenes. When Albert Hallam retired in 1975, Graham Tongue became the head modeller at the Beswick Studio under Harry Sales, newly appointed as design manager.

Harry Sales was primarily a graphic artist and he dreamed up many new ideas for Bunnykins figures, which Graham Tongue and others modelled during the 1980s. He created a new adult audience for Bunnykins with his witty sporting subjects, for example *Jogging Bunnykins* and *Bogey Bunnykins*, and as collector interest grew, he began to design special commission,s such as *Uncle Sam* and *Collector Bunnykins*. At the same time, he was responsible for the continued development of the Beatrix Potter range, which was becoming increasingly difficult as the most popular characters had already been modelled. Favourites, such as *Peter Rabbit* and *Jemima Puddleduck*, were introduced in new poses, and he came up with the idea of double figures, for example *Mr Benjamin Bunny and Peter Rabbit* and *Tabitha Twitchet and Miss Moppet*.

As well as developing the established figure collections, Harry Sales delved into lots of other children's books for inspiration. He re-interpreted the timeless characters from classic tales such as *Alice's Adventures in Wonderland* and *Wind in the Willows*, and he worked from contemporary picture books, notably Joan Walsh Anglund's *A Friend is Someone Who Likes You* and Norman Thelwell's *Angels on Horseback*. Whenever possible, Harry liaised closely with the originators of the characters he portrayed. He spent many happy hours of research at Thelwell's studio, studying his cartoons of shaggy ponies with comical riders, and he also worked with Alfred Bestall, the illustrator of the *Rupert Bear* adventures in the *Daily Express* newspaper before embarking on this series in 1980.

With their outstanding reputation for developing character animals it is not surprising that Royal Doulton artists were invited to work on the publishing sensation of the 1980s, the Brambly Hedge stories by Jill Barklem. Within three years of their launch the spring, summer, autumn and winter stories had been reprinted 11 times, translated into ten languages, and had sold in excess of a million copies. Readers young and old were captivated by the enchanting world of the Brambly Hedge mice, as indeed was Harry Sales, whose job it was to recreate the characters in the ceramic medium. In his own words, "The first time I read the books and studied the illustrations I felt that I was experiencing something quite unique. Over a period of many years designing for the pottery industry one develops an awareness, a 'feeling' for that something special. Brambly Hedge had this."

Ideas flowed quickly and eight leading characters were chosen from the seasonal stories for the initial collection, which was launched in 1983. Such was the response that they were soon joined by six more subjects, making a total of 14 by 1986, when Harry left the company. Graham Tongue succeeded him as design manager and has continued to add new Brambly Hedge figures from the original stories on a regular basis. Miss Barklem's later titles, *The Secret Staircase, The High Hills* and *The Sea Story*, have also provided inspiration for some of the more recent figures; for example, *Mr and Mrs Saltapple* supply the Brambly Hedge community with salt in *The Sea Story*.

Encouraged by the amazing success of the Brambly Hedge collection, Royal Doulton's marketing executives were soon considering other new storybook characters. Like millions of TV viewers, they were spellbound by the magical film, *The Snowman*, which was first screened in 1982. Based on the illustrated book of the same name by Raymond Briggs, the animated film about a snowman who comes to life has become traditional Christmas entertainment in many parts of the world. The absence of words gives the tale a haunting quality, and there is hardly a dry eye in the house when the little boy, James, awakes to find his Snowman friend has melted away after an exciting night exploring each other's worlds. Fortunately the SNOWMAN™ lives on in more durable form in the Royal Doulton collection. Again Harry Sales was given the challenge of transforming this amorphous character into ceramic, whilst remaining faithful to Briggs' original soft crayon drawings. He succeeded in this difficult task by adding additional curves to the contours of the figures which gives them a life-like appearance. The first four figures were ready and approved by Raymond Briggs in 1985, and the collection grew steadily until 1990, latterly under the direction of Graham Tongue.

So far the 1990s has seen Graham Tongue and his team of artists developing the Beatrix Potter and Bunnykins collections for two major anniversaries—the 100th birthday of *Peter Rabbit* and the diamond jubilee of Bunnykins in 1994. Also in 1994, the centenary of the Beswick factory was marked with the launch of the *Pig Promenade*, featuring a special commemorative backstamp.

This series is just one of three new collections of novelty figures, and it is refreshing to see this traditional type of Beswick ware being revitalised by a new generation of artists. Amanda Hughes-Lubeck and Warren Platt created the LITTLE LOVABLES™, a series of cute clowns with special messages, such as "Good Luck" and "Congratulations," and they also worked with Martyn Alcock on the collection of ENGLISH COUNTRY FOLK™, which has been very well received.

The collecting of Beatrix Potter and Bunnykins figures has reached epidemic proportions in recent years, and there is now a growing awareness of the desirability of all their storybook cousins, hence the need for this much expanded price guide.

COLLECTING BEATRIX POTTER FIGURES

A number of factors have combined recently to make Beatrix Potter figures the "hottest" collectables of the 1990s. The 100th birthday of *Peter Rabbit* was celebrated amidst a storm of publicity in 1993, and the first reference book on the Beswick and Royal Albert figures was launched to coincide with all the celebrations. In addition, the centenary of the John Beswick factory in 1994 focused a lot of collector attention on their products.

The market has been stimulated by recent withdrawals from the range—12 were announced at the end of 1993, and six at the end of 1994, making a total of 30 retired figures to date. Prices are rocketing for the early discontinued figures, and most collectors will need a bank loan to purchase *Duchess with Flowers*, the first Beatrix Potter figure to be retired, if indeed they are lucky enough to find one for sale.

Ever since the Beswick factory launched their Beatrix Potter collection in 1948, most of the figures have been bought as gifts for children. However, many young fans have grown up to find they have some very valuable figures, with early modelling and backstamp variations, and they have begun collecting in earnest to fill the gaps and find the rarities. Figures marked with a Beswick backstamp are most in demand, as this trademark was replaced with the Royal Albert backstamp in 1989. The Royal Albert factory, another famous name in the Doulton group, produces all the Beatrix Potter tableware, and the change of backstamps was made for distribution reasons. The most desirable Beswick marks are the gold varieties, which predate 1972, and these are often found on early modelling or colour variations, which also attract a premium price, for example, *Mrs Rabbit* with her umbrella sticking out and *Mr Benjamin Bunny* with his pipe protruding.

As well as seeking out discontinued figures and rare variations, it is advisable to keep up to date with new models as they are introduced. A complete Beatrix Potter figure collection will encompass 96 of the standard-size models, around three inches tall, and eight large models, which are about twice the size. *Peter Rabbit*, the first of these large size models, was launched in 1993 with a special commemorative backstamp from the John Beswick studio, and it changed in 1994 to the standard Royal Albert mark.

If owning all the Beatrix Potter figures is beyond the realms of possibility, whether for financial or display limitations, then why not focus on particular types of animals or characters from your favourite tales. There are twenty mice figures to find, a dozen cat characters and more than twenty rabbits, including seven portraits of *Peter Rabbit* to date. There are also discontinued character jugs, relief modelled plaques and a ceramic display stand to look out for, so happy hunting.

COLLECTING BUNNYKINS FIGURES

The diamond jubilee of Bunnykins brought the famous rabbit family into the limelight once again, and a special *60th Anniversary Bunnykins*, proudly carrying a birthday cake, was just one of eight new figures released in 1994. Even more are planned for 1995, and this wide variety of introductions is indicative of today's tremendous enthusiasm for collecting Bunnykins. When the DB range was launched in 1972, most of the figures were purchased to amuse young children, but the sporting characters of the 1980s began to appeal to adults and, in many cases, exchanging whimsical gifts developed into serious collecting.

Harry Sales drawing for *Collector Bunnykins*

The golden jubilee celebrations in 1984 introduced Bunnykins to an even wider audience, and led to the first collectors book, published by Richard Dennis. Fans were introduced to the entire range of nurseryware and figures, including the six large-size models from 1939, which are extremely hard to find. Apart from these elusive models, it was relatively easy to form a complete collection of figures in the mid 1980s, as the DB range consisted of just 28 models with only four withdrawals. *Autumn Days*, *Springtime*, *The Artist* and *Grandpa's Story*, withdrawn in 1982 and 1983, are now very sought after on the secondary market, but subsequent developments have generated much rarer characters. In 1986, Royal Doulton USA ordered new colourways of *Mr and Mrs Easter Bunnykins* to sell at a programme of artist demonstrations, and these are now extremely difficult to find. Similarly, the two special colourways of *Bedtime Bunnykins*, made for D. H. Holmes and Belks department stores in 1987 and 1988, are now increasing in price as serious collectors try to get hold of them.

Although most Bunnykins characters are modelled with young children in mind, there have been several subjects exclusively for collectors, notably *Collector Bunnykins* which was commissioned by the International Collectors Club in 1987. As it was only offered for a six month period, it is now one of the rarest models in the DB range. *The Royal Doulton Collectors Band,* featuring the first limite- edition Bunnykins figures, was launched at the London Doulton Fair in 1990, and since then there have been several limited pieces for exclusive distribution and special occasions. The overwhelming response to these special commissions was highlighted last year when the *Sergeant Mountie Bunnykins* sold out within hours of its launch at the Canadian Doulton show. Similarly, many of the limited editions commissioned by UK International Ceramics are now fully subscribed.

With this in mind, it is a good idea to buy the new Bunnykins figures as soon as they are issued. Royal Doulton have now allocated more than 150 DB numbers and, although a few intervening numbers have not been issued, notably *Ballet Bunnykins,* DB 44, committed collectors now have quite a challenge to find them all. Figures are now regularly withdrawn from the range, adding to the excitement of the chase and, like many fellow collectors, you can always dream of finding all the rare 1939 models!

COLLECTING BRAMBLY HEDGE FIGURES

Since their introduction in 1983, the Brambly Hedge mice have overrun households in many parts of the world. They are scurrying about the shelves as Royal Doulton figures and even climbing up the walls on decorative plates. Far from being undesirable, these particular mice are considered indispensable members of the family. Children frequently receive them as gifts from doting grandparents, but adults have also been seduced by the cosy, timeless mouse world which Jill Barklem has created. The mood of rustic nostalgia has all been painstakingly researched. The interiors of the field mice homes are of the sort common in English farmhouses at the end of the 19th century, and the food served is genuine country fare, based on old recipes and tasted in Jill Barklem's kitchen. The Brambly Hedge residents were all expertly drawn with the aid of her two mouse models, a keen understanding of zoology and a knowledge of historical costume.

The same attention to detail went into the Royal Doulton figures designed by Harry Sales. As he explains, "One important feature in the concept was that I chose poses which, when the figures are together, appear to be reacting to one another. I can imagine the fun children and the young at heart will have arranging the figures in conversational situations." Essentially this sums up the collectability of the Brambly Hedge mice, and the size of the series means they can all still be displayed effectively together on one shelf. To date there have been 25 little figures, and all are still relatively affordable, although the eight withdrawals are beginning to have an impact on the secondary market. There is one unusual modelling variation to look out for, as *Mr Toadflax's* tail was altered shortly after its introduction.

COLLECTING SNOWMAN FIGURES

The seasonal appeal of the Snowman has tended to limit his collectability, as most purchases are made around Christmas time, and he is more popular in areas which regularly experience snow. Having said this, for some fans the wintry connotations are overshadowed by the inherent quality and humour of the models and there are keen collectors in sunny Florida as well as in Australia, where beach barbecues are typical Christmas celebrations.

Between 1985 and 1990, young children regularly received the new Snowman models in their Christmas stockings, and the characters have been widely used as holiday decorations. Like the Brambly Hedge models, they were designed to interact, and the little figure of *James,* gazing up in wonder can be positioned with various Snowman characters, whilst the band works very well as a separate display grouping. There are 19 figures and two musical boxes to collect and, as the range has now all been withdrawn, they can now be quite difficult to locate. After a gap of four years, a new type of Snowman collectable was launched in July 1994, in the form of a miniature character jug by Martyn Alcock. Perhaps this will be the catalyst to a renewed interest in the Snowman collection.

COLLECTING STORYBOOK CHARACTERS

The Beatrix Potter, Brambly Hedge and Snowman stories have already been discussed in some detail, as there are so many figures to collect in each of the categories. However, the Beswick artists have also sought inspiration in other children's stories, some better known than others.

The American author-illustrator, Joan Walsh Anglund, enjoyed quite a vogue in the 1960s following the publication of *A Friend is Someone Who Likes You* (1958). Three of her drawings of cute children with minimal features were modelled by Albert Hallam for the Beswick range in 1969, but they were withdrawn soon after, making them extremely hard to find today.

The bizarre cast of characters from *Alice's Adventures in Wonderland* has offered a lot more scope for collectors. First published in 1865, this classic tale has entertained generations of young readers and inspired many artistic interpretations. In the early 1900s, Doulton's Lambeth artists modelled some fantastic creatures from the tale, notably the pig-like *Rath* from the "Jabberwocky" poem. The Burslem studio designed an extensive series of nurseryware and, more recently, a collection of character jugs based on the original illustrations by Sir John Tenniel, who firmly fixed the appearance of the Wonderland characters in the public imagination. Harry Sales also consulted the Tenniel illustrations in 1973 when designing Beswick's ALICE IN WONDERLAND™ series. The resulting 11 figures faithfully capture the spirit of the book and remained a popular set in the range until 1983.

Curiously the figures inspired by another great children's classic, *Wind in the Willows,* did not have the same appeal. Christina Thwaites, a young book illustrator, was commissioned to produce designs for a collection of wall plates and tea wares, and her watercolours of Mr Toad, Ratty, Mole, Badger and others were interpreted by the Beswick modellers. Four figures were launched in 1987 and two more in 1988 as part of a co-ordinated giftware range with the Royal Albert backstamp, but they were withdrawn in 1989. Consequently *Portly* and *Weasel*, the later introductions, were only made for one year, and will no doubt prove particularly hard to find in the future.

With the WIND IN THE WILLOWS™ collection, the Royal Doulton artists have come full circle, reflecting the enthusiasm of their predecessors at Lambeth, notably Francis Pope who modelled two superb figures of Mr Toad shortly after the book was published. Obviously storybook characters, particularly animals in human guises, have timeless appeal.

COLLECTING CARTOON CHARACTERS

Cartoon characters, whether they be from animated films or comic book strips, are becoming a popular field for collectors. The forthcoming book on the subject, together with future introductions, such as *Tom and Jerry*, will surely generate even more interest. Now is the time to start collecting, if you have not already done so.

The characters from David Hand's Animal Land are virtually unknown today, but following their film debut in 1948, they were sufficiently well known to inspire Beswick's first series of cartoon figures. Modelled in 1949 and withdrawn in 1955, *Zimmy the Lion* and his seven friends now have a different kind of notoriety, stealing the show when they come up for auction.

In contrast, Mickey Mouse is the best known cartoon character in the world. Within a year of his 1928 screen debut in *Steamboat Willie*, his image was being used to endorse children's products, and by the 1950s there were more than 3,000 different Mickey Mouse items, including plates, dolls, watches and clothes. With all this merchandising activity, it is not surprising that the Beswick studio sought a license for portraying Mickey and his friends in ceramic.

A range of nurseyware was launched in 1954, along with figures of *Mickey* and his girlfriend *Minnie*, *Pluto* his dog and his crazy friends *Goofy* and *Donald Duck*. Characters from some of Walt Disney's feature-length cartoons completed the original WALT DISNEY CHARACTERS™ set of 12 figures. *Peter Pan*, the newest Disney hit in 1953, inspired four characters, *Peter* himself, *Tinkerbell*, *Smee* and *Nana*, whilst the classic *Pinocchio* (1940) provided the puppet hero and his insect conscience *Jiminy Cricket*. Surprisingly only *Thumper* was modelled from another favourite film, *Bambi* (1942), although the baby deer appears on the tableware designs. The response to the initial Disney collection encouraged the Beswick factory to launch a second set the following year, featuring *Snow White and the Seven Dwarfs* from Disney's first feature symphony. All the Disney characterisations are superb, making them extremely desirable amongst collectors of Beswick and Disneyana and they are all hard to find, even though they were produced until 1967.

The 1960s saw the rise of a new Disney star, Winnie the Pooh, who became a very popular merchandising character after his cartoon debut in 1966. The Beswick factory was quick off the mark, launching an initial collection of six characters from the film in 1968, followed by two more in 1971. "The Bear of Little Brain" originated in bedtime stories about nursery toys told by AA Milne to his son Christopher Robin in the 1920s, and he was visualised in the resulting books by the illustrator E.H. Shepard. Royal Doulton recently launched a range of nurseryware with scenes adapted from the *Winnie the Pooh* books and more developments are planned in the future.

The massive marketing campaigns for Disney characters have made them household names all over the world. British cartoon characters, by comparison, are less well known internationally. The *Daily Express* newspaper was slow to capitalise on the success of Rupert the Bear, who has been the star of their children's comic strip since 1920. Originated by Mary Tourtel, the Rupert stories were enlivened by Alfred Bestall who took over the daily drawings in 1935. Rupert enjoys the most extraordinary adventures with his friends Bill the Badger, Algy Pug and Pong-Ping, always returning safely to his comfortable family home in Nutwood. Rupert Bear annuals sold in millions from the mid 1930s, and his exploits were adapted for TV in the 1970s, but his following is essentially British. No doubt it was for this reason that the five figures in the RUPERT THE BEAR™ collection, designed by Harry Sales in 1980, were relatively short lived.

A similar fate befell the THELWELL™ figures, which were in production from 1981 to 1989. Norman Thelwell was a humorous illustrator for *Punch* magazine, who made his reputation with comical observations of young riders and their mounts. *Angels on Horseback*, published in 1957, was the first compilation of his successful cartoons, and many other popular books followed. Thelwell worked closely with Harry Sales to create the most effective figures, both in ceramic and resin, and the results are guaranteed to raise a smile without breaking the bank.

After a gap of nearly 15 years, famous cartoon characters are back on the drawing board at the Royal Doulton studios once again. *Denis the Menace* and *Desperate Dan*, stars of the long-established children's comics, *The Beano* and *The Dandy*, have been immortalised as character jugs. This is the first time large-size character jugs have been used for portraying cartoons, although there are similarities to the set of six THUNDERBIRDS™ busts modelled by jug designer Bill Harper to celebrate the 30th anniversary of this children's TV show in 1992.

COLLECTING CHARACTER ANIMALS

In the 1880s Doulton's first artist, George Tinworth, was modelling groups of mice engaged in popular human pastimes, and nearly a century later Kitty McBride did much the same thing with her *Happy Mice*. The appeal of these anthropomorphic creatures is timeless, and collectors have responded with enthusiasm from Victorian times to the present day. Admittedly, developing a taste for Tinworth's sense of humour will prove very expensive, with models costing several hundreds of pounds each, but the KITTY MCBRIDE™ whimsical mice are still relatively affordable.

Kitty McBride was a writer and illustrator who began to model little clay figures of mice in 1960. Initially they were sold through a London dealer, but when she could not keep up with the demand she asked the Beswick factory to produce 11 of them commercially, which they did between 1975 and 1983.

The Beswick studio has had a considerable reputation for character animals since the launch of the Beatrix Potter collection in 1948. However, the modellers have not only interpreted illustrations from famous books, from time to time they have envisaged their own comical creatures. Arthur Gredington modelled an amusing *Cat Orchestra* in 1945, Jan Granoska produced her colourful *Monkey Band* in 1952 and Albert Hallam was responsible for a succession of animals with human expressions in the late 1960s. Similar humanising traits can be found in the LITTLE LIKABLES™ collection, which was produced briefly in the mid 1980s. Robert Tabbenor's animals play up the humour of their situation, notably the carefree frog, *Watching the World Go By*, whilst Diane Griffiths takes a more sentimental approach, using human feelings to describe her cartoon-like animals.

The fun has continued in recent years with a collection of footballer cats, produced in 1987 only, and the on-going series of English Country Folk, depicting appropriate animals with human manners and costumes. However, the last laugh is reserved for the new Pig Promenade. The absurdity of seven different breeds of pigs playing musical instruments makes this one of the most hilarious series of character animals.

MAKING STORYBOOK CHARACTERS

All the current storybook characters are made at the John Beswick factory in Longton, which became part of the Royal Doulton group in 1969. They have over fifty years' experience in the production of humorous figures and character animals, and essentially the methods have not changed since the earliest days of the Beatrix Potter figures.

First of all the designer has to familiarise himself thoroughly with the character to be portrayed, reading the story and studying the illustration. Having chosen the most suitable pose for interpretation in ceramic, he will produce reference drawings for the modeller. Often he can only see one side of the character in the original illustration, so he has to improvise for his three-dimensional model.

In consultation with the designer, the modeller will create the figure in modelling clay, and if satisfactory, a set of master moulds will be made in plaster of Paris. The number of mould parts will depend on the complexity of the figure, and sometimes the head and arms have to be moulded separately. Two or three prototype figures will be cast from the master mould for colour trials and subsequent approval by the original artist or his agent.

In the case of the Beatrix Potter figures, all the models are scrutinised by the licensing agents, Copyrights, working on behalf of Miss Potter's original publishers, Frederick Warne. Raymond Briggs, who was responsible for the Snowman, is generally quite relaxed about letting experts in other media interpret his drawings. He thought Royal Doulton's models were marvellous and really captured the spirit of the story, although he maintained he would "jolly well say so" if he thought they had got it wrong! Jill Barklem, the creator of Brambly Hedge, likes to get very involved in the licensing of her characters, and design manager Harry Sales spent a lot of time working with her on the finer points of detail. Sometimes slight modifications need to be made to the model or the colour scheme before the figure is approved by all concerned.

The next stage is to produce plaster of Paris working moulds from the master, and supplies are sent to the casting department. An earthenware body is used to cast all the character figures produced at the John Beswick studio, and it is poured into the mould in liquid form, known as slip. The moisture in the slip is absorbed into the plaster of Paris moulds and a "skin" of clay forms the interior.

Once the clay has set to the required thickness, the excess clay is poured out and the mould is carefully dismantled. Any separate mould parts, such as projecting arms, will be joined on at this stage using slip as an adhesive, and the seams will be gently sponged away. The figure is then allowed to dry slowly before it goes for its first firing. The high temperature in the kiln drives out the moisture in the body and the figure shrinks by about 1/12th of its original size, forming a hard "biscuit" body.

Skilled decorators will paint the figure, using special under-glaze ceramic colours. They work from an approved colour sample and great care is taken to match the colours to the original book illustrations. A second firing hardens on the colour before the figure is coated with a solution of liquid glaze. When the figure is fired in the glost kiln, it emerges with a shiny transparent finish which enhances and permanently protects the vibrant colours underneath. After a final inspection, the figures are dispatched to china shops all over the world where they will capture the hearts of collectors young and old.

RESIN FIGURES

Several collectables manufacturers began experimenting with new sculptural materials in the 1980s and developed different types of resin bodies that allow more intricately modelled detail than conventional ceramic processes. Royal Doulton launched their new "bonded ceramic body" in 1984, and two storybook collections were included in their Beswick Studio Sculptures, as the range was known. Seven subjects were chosen from the *Tales of Beatrix Potter* and two from the Thelwell series, but production was short lived, despite the minute detailing of the animals' fur and the tiny pebbles and grasses in their habitat, which would have been impossible to achieve in traditional earthenware. Royal Doulton ceased production of resin at the end of 1985, but they have occasionally commission 12 little Beswick Bears which were only available in 1993.

BUYING CURRENT AND DISCONTINUED STORYBOOK CHARACTERS

The Royal Doulton Company owns many well-known china factories, including John Beswick, Royal Albert and Royal Doulton itself, and different trademarks are used for historical reasons or depending on the type of product. The Bunnykins, Brambly Hedge and Snowman collections feature the Royal Doulton backstamp, the Pig Promenade and English Country Folk carry a Beswick backstamp, whilst the Beatrix Potter figures, originally part of the Beswick range, are now marked Royal Albert. All these varied collections are produced at the John Beswick factory in Longton, Stoke-on-Trent, and models still being made at the factory today are referred to as "current." Most of the current storybook figures can be purchased in specialist china shops or from mail-order companies specialising in collectables. However, some Bunnykins figures have been commissioned for exclusive distribution, notably the special editions for UK International Ceramics, and these are available direct from this company in the UK or from their appointed agents overseas.

Up-to-date information about new introductions to the storybook collections is included in *Gallery* magazine, which is published quarterly by the Royal Doulton International Collectors Club. The Club regularly commissions exclusive collectables for its membership, and Bunnykins figures have been featured in the past. Members also receive information about withdrawals to the collection in the various branch newsletters.

Once a piece has been withdrawn from production, it is referred to as "discontinued" or "retired," and it enters the secondary market. Many specialist Royal Doulton dealers around the world carry discontinued storybook characters. Some have shops or showrooms, but most sell by mail order and exhibit regularly at antique shows. Some of the more expensive Bunnykins and Beatrix Potter figures are now being sold at auction, notably *Duchess with Flowers*. Most storybook characters do not yet qualify for the minimum lot price but it is still worth watching out for group lots at auctions or estate sales, in case some of the character animals have been included. Perhaps a rare Beatrix Potter or Bunnykins colourway will not be recognised as such!

WHERE TO BUY

Discontinued storybook figures can be found in antique shops, markets and fairs, as well as at auction houses. Specialist dealers in these figures attend many of the venues and events below.

UNITED KINGDOM

Auction Houses

Phillips
101 New Bond Street
London W1

Christie's South Kensington
85 Old Brompton Road
London SW5

Bonhams
Montpelier Street
London SW7

Sotheby's
Summer's Place
Billingshurst, West Sussex

Louis Taylor
Percy Street
Hanley, Stoke-on-Trent

Peter Wilson
Victoria Gallery
Market Street
Nantwich, Cheshire

Antique Fairs

U.K. Doulton Collectors Fair
The Queensway Hall
Civic Centre
Dunstable, Bedfordshire

Stafford International Doulton Fair
Stafford County Showground
Stafford

Doulton and Beswick Collectors Fair
National Motorcycle Museum
Meriden, Birmingham

Antique Markets

Portobello Road Market
London W11
Saturday only

New Caledonian Market
Bermondsey Square
London SE1
Friday morning

Alfie's Antique Market
13-25 Church Street
London NW8
Tuesday-Saturday

Camden Passage Market
(of Upper Street)
London N1
Wednesday and Saturday

U.S.A.

Auction Houses

Phillips New York
406 East 79th Street
New York, NY 10021

Antique Fairs

Florida Doulton Convention
Guest Quarters Suite Hotel
Cypress Creek
555 NW 62nd Street
Fort Lauderdale, Florida 33309

Doulton Show
Sheraton Poste House
Cherry Hill, New Jersey

Doulton Show
Holiday Inn
Independence, Ohio

CANADA

Auction Houses

D & J Ritchie Inc.
288 King Street East
Toronto, Ontario, M5A 1K4

Antique Shows

The Canadian Royal Doulton & Beswick Collectors Fair
Holiday Inn Crowne Plaze
Toronto Airport
970 Dixon Road
Etobicoke, Ontario

Antique Markets

Harbourfront Antique Market
390 Queen's Quay West
Toronto, Ontario
(Tuesday - Sunday)

PLACES TO VISIT

John Beswick Factory Tour
Gold Street
Longton, Stoke-on-Trent
ST3 2JP
For opening times and tour information telephone
(0782) 292292

Royal Doulton Factory Tour
and Sir Henry Doulton Gallery
Nile Street
Burslem, Stoke-on-Trent
For opening times and tour information telephone
(0782) 744766

CLUBS AND SOCIETIES

The Royal Doulton International Collectors Club was founded in 1980 to provide an information service on all aspects of the company's products, past and present. The club's magazine, *Gallery*, is published four times a year, and local branches also publish newsletters. There are also several regional groups in the U.S.A. that meet for lectures and other events, and some publish newsletters. Contact the U.S.A. branch for further information.

Headquarters and U.K. Branch

Royal Doulton
Minton House
London Road
Stoke-on-Trent ST4 7QD

Australian Branch

Royal Doulton Australia Pty Ltd.
17-23 Merriwa Street
Gordon NSW 2072

Canadian Branch

Royal Doulton Canada Inc.
850 Progress Road
Scarborough, Ontario M1H 3C4

New Zealand Branch

Royal Doulton
P.O. Box 2059
Auckland

U.S.A. Branch

Royal Doulton U.S.A. Inc
P.O. Box 1815
Somerset, New Jersey 08873

FURTHER READING

Storybook Figures

Royal Doulton Bunnykins Figures, by Louise Irvine
Bunnykins Collectors Book, by Louise Irvine
Beatrix Potter Figures, edited by Louise Irvine
The Beswick Price Guide, by Harvey May

Animals, Figures and Character Jugs

Royal Doulton Figures, by Desmond Eyles, Louise Irvine and Valerie Baynton
The Charlton Standard Catalogue of Royal Doulton Animals, by Jean Dale
The Charlton Standard Catalogue of Royal Doulton Figurines, by Jean Dale
The Charlton Standard Catalogue of Royal Doulton Jugs, by Jean Dale
Collecting Character and Toby Jugs, by Jocelyn Lukins
Collecting Doulton Animals, by Jocelyn Lukins
Doulton Flambé Animals, by Jocelyn Lukins
The Character Jug Collectors Handbook, by Kevin Pearson
The Doulton Figure Collectors Handbook, by Kevin Pearson

General

Discovering Royal Doulton, by Michael Doulton
The Doulton Story, by Paul Atterbury and Louise Irvine
Royal Doulton Series Wares, by Louise Irvine (Vols. 1-4)
Limited Edition Loving Cups and Jugs, by Louise Irvine and Richard Dennis
Doulton for the Collector, by Jocelyn Lukins
Doulton Kingsware Flasks, by Jocelyn Lukins
Doulton Burslem Advertising Wares, by Jocelyn Lukins
Doulton Lambeth Advertising Wares, by Jocelyn Lukins
The Doulton Lambeth Wares, by Desmond Eyles
The Doulton Burslem Wares, by Desmond Eyles
Hannah Barlow, by Peter Rose
George Tinworth, by Peter Rose
Sir Henry Doulton Biography, by Edmund Gosse
Phillips Collectors Guide, by Catherine Braithwaite
Royal Doulton, by Jennifer Queree
Collecting Doulton Magazine, published by Francis Joseph, edited by Doug Pinchin

ALICE IN WONDERLAND

2476
ALICE™

Designer:	Albert Hallam and Graham Tongue
Height:	4 3/4", 12.1 cm
Colour:	Blue dress, white apron and red trim
Issued:	1973-1983

Beswick Number	*Price U.S. $*	*Can. $*	*U.K. £*	*Aust. $*
2476	450.00	525.00	245.00	700.00

2477
WHITE RABBIT™

Designer:	Graham Tongue
Height:	4 3/4", 12.1 cm
Colour:	Brown coat, yellow waistcoat
Issued:	1973-1983

Beswick Number	*Price U.S. $*	*Can. $*	*U.K. £*	*Aust. $*
2477	450.00	525.00	245.00	700.00

2478
MOCK TURTLE™

Designer:	Graham Tongue
Height:	4 1/4", 10.8 cm
Colour:	Browns and grey
Issued:	1973-1983

Beswick Number	*Price U.S. $*	*Can. $*	*U.K. £*	*Aust. $*
2478	300.00	350.00	125.00	200.00

2479
MAD HATTER™

Designer: Albert Hallam
Height: 4 1/4", 10.8 cm
Colour: Burgundy coat; yellow and blue checked trousers; yellow and red bow tie; grey hat
Issued: 1973-1983

Beswick Number	*U.S. $*	*Price Can. $*	*U.K. £*	*Aust. $*
2479	375.00	425.00	200.00	700.00

2480
CHESHIRE CAT™

Designer: Albert Hallam and Graham Tongue
Height: 1 1/2", 3.8 cm
Colour: Tabby
Issued: 1973-1982

Beswick. Number	*U.S. $*	*Can. $*	*Price U.K. £*	*Aust. $*
2480	800.00	900.00	500.00	1,000.00

2485
GRYPHON™

Designer: Albert Hallam
Height: 3 1/4", 8.3 cm
Colour: Browns and greens
Issued: 1973-1983

Beswick Number	*U.S. $*	*Price Can. $*	*U.K. £*	*Aust. $*
2485	300.00	350.00	80.00	200.00

2489
KING OF HEARTS™

Designer: Graham Tongue
Height: 3 3/4", 9.5 cm
Colour: Burgundy, yellow, white, blue and green
Issued: 1973-1983

Beswick Number	*Price* *U.S. $*	*Can. $*	*U.K. £*	*Aust. $*
2489	125.00	140.00	55.00	200.00

2490
QUEEN OF HEARTS™

Designer: Graham Tongue
Height: 4", 10.1 cm
Colour: Blue, green, yellow, white and burgundy
Issued: 1973-1983

Beswick Number	*Price* *U.S. $*	*Can. $*	*U.K. £*	*Aust. $*
2490	125.00	140.00	55.00	200.00

2545
DODO™

Designer: David Lyttleton
Height: 4", 10.1 cm
Colour: Browns and greens
Issued: 1975-1983

Beswick Number	*Price* *U.S. $*	*Can. $*	*U.K. £*	*Aust. $*
2545	325.00	375.00	150.00	400.00

2546
FISH FOOTMAN™

Designer: David Lyttleton
Height: 4 3/4", 14.6 cm
Colour: Blue, gold, white and brown
Issued: 1975-1983

ALICE SERIES
"Fish Footman"
BESWICK
MADE IN ENGLAND
© ROYAL DOULTON TABLEWARE LTD 1976
REGISTRATION APPLIED FOR

Beswick Number	*U.S. $*	*Price Can. $*	*U.K. £*	*Aust. $*
2546	275.00	325.00	160.00	500.00

Photograph not available at press time

2547
FROG FOOTMAN™

Designer: David Lyttleton
Height: 4 1/4", 10.8 cm
Colour: Maroon jacket with yellow trim and blue trousers
Issued: 1975-1983

ALICE SERIES
"Frog Footman"
BESWICK
MADE IN ENGLAND
© ROYAL DOULTON TABLEWARE LTD 1976
REGISTRATION APPLIED FOR

Beswick Number	*U.S. $*	*Price Can. $*	*U.K. £*	*Aust. $*
2547	275.00	325.00	190.00	450.00

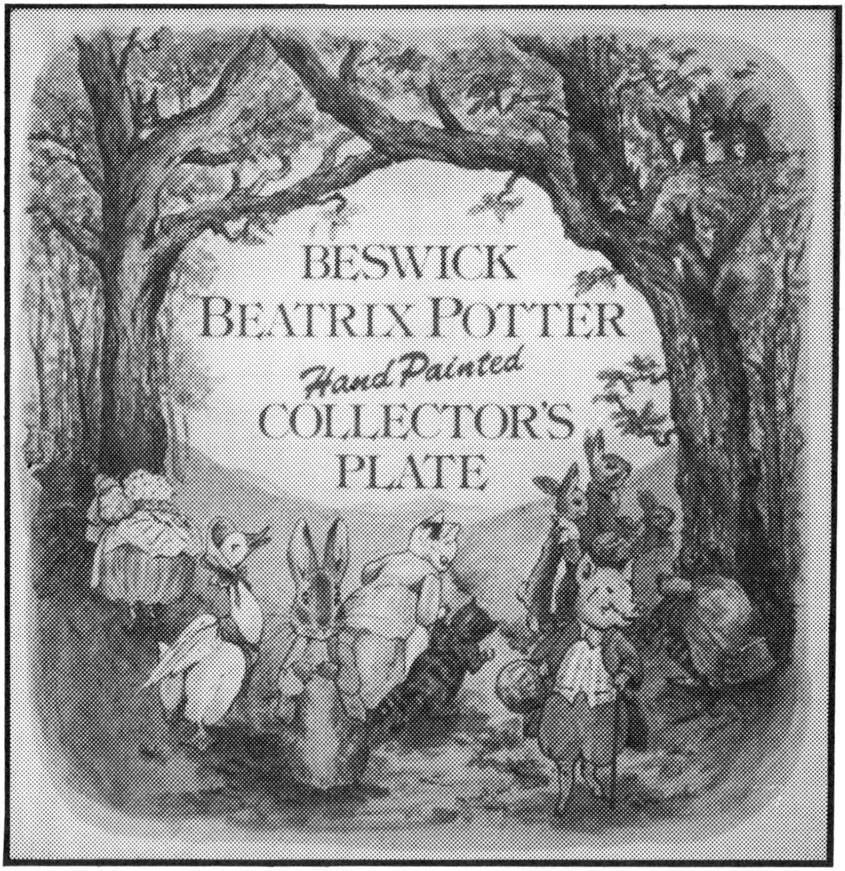
BESWICK
BEATRIX POTTER
Hand Painted
COLLECTOR'S
PLATE

BEATRIX POTTER

P

Painting a portrait

BEATRIX POTTER BACKSTAMPS

BP-1. BESWICK GOLD CIRCLE BACKSTAMP 1948 -1954

BP-1 was used on 21 figures between 1948 and 1954. There are two varieties of this backstamp, the first a "circle" and the second a modification of the circle. The second due to the small base on three figures, Miss Moppet, Mrs. Rabbit and Tailor of Gloucester, had the backstamp circle flattened and the "copyright" in script lettering.

The following is a list of figures which will be found with a BP-1 backstamp:

Benjamin Bunny, first version
Flopsy, Mopsy and Cottontail
Foxy Whiskered Gentleman
Hunca Munca
Jemima Puddleduck
Johnny Townmouse
Lady Mouse
Little Pig Robinson, first version
Miss Moppet, first version
Mr. Jeremy Fisher
Mrs. Rabbit, first version
Mrs. Tiggy Winkle, first version
Mrs. Tittlemouse
Peter Rabbit, first version
Ribby
Samuel Whiskers
Squirrel Nutkin
Tailor of Gloucester
Timmy Tiptoes
Timmy Willie
Tom Kitten

BP-2. BESWICK GOLD OVAL BACKSTAMP 1955-1972

The gold oval was in use for 18 years, between 1955 and 1972, and it was used on 38 figures during the "gold oval period". Pig-Wig, introduced in 1972, was the last in line for the gold oval backstamp, and in some quarters they still doubt that it officially exists.

The following is a list of figures which will be found with a BP-2 backstamp:

Amiable Guinea Pig
Anna Maria
Appley Dappley, first version
Aunt Pettitoes
Benjamin Bunny, first version
Cecily Parsley, first version
Cousin Ribby
Duches (with flowers)
Flopsy, Mopsy and Cottontail
Foxy Whiskered Gentleman
Goody Tiptoes
Hunca Munca
Jemima Puddleduck
Johnny Townmouse
Lady Mouse
Little Pig Robinson, first version
Miss Moppet, first version
Mr. Benjamin Bunny, first version
Mr. Jeremy Fisher
Mrs. Flopsy Bunny
Mrs. Rabbit, first version
Mrs. Tiggy Winkle, first version
Mrs. Tittlemouse
Old Mr. Brown
Old Woman who lived in a Shoe
Peter Rabbit, first version
Pickles
Pigling Bland
Pig-Wig
Ribby
Samuel Whiskers
Squirrel Nutkin
Tabitha Twitchit
Tailor of Gloucester
Timmy Tiptoes
Timmy Willie
Tom Kitten
Tommy Brock, first version

BP-3. BESWICK BROWN LINE BACKSTAMP 1973-1988

In use between the years 1973 and 1988, this brown line (Beswick and England are in line) backstamps appear on 69 figures, including the different versions. The brown line backstamp saw three major revisions during the 16 years it was in use.

A. — Potter's; No date; Copyright 1973-1974

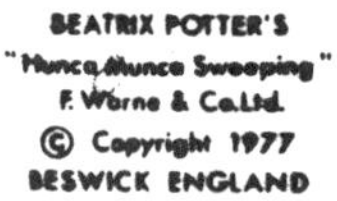

B. — Potter's; Date; Copyright 1974-1985

C. — Potter (no "s"); Date; Copyright 1985-1988

BP-4. BESWICK DOULTON BROWN SIGNATURE BACKSTAMP 1988-1989

This era saw the Beswick backstamp converted to the Royal Doulton backstamp. The connection with Beswick was kept by the addition of the John Beswick signature to the backstamp. In use for a year to a year and a half, this is the shortest time period for a backstamp covering the complete range of figures in issue.

BP-5. ROYAL ALBERT GOLD CROWN BACKSTAMP 1989

The gold backstamp was re-instituted for 1989 to mark the change from the Doulton/Beswick backstamps to Royal Albert. It was used on only 6 figures:

Benjamin Bunny
Flopsy, Mopsy and Cottontail
Hunca Munca
Jemima Puddleduck
Mrs. Rabbit and Bunnies
Peter Rabbit

BP-6. ROYAL ALBERT BROWN CROWN BACKSTAMP 1989 TO DATE

There are two known varieties of this backstamp with and without, the crown. For cross reference see "Beatrix Potter Figures" backstamp B-11.

BP-7. BESWICK BROWN OVAL BACKSTAMP 1993

One variation of this backstamp is the 100th anniversary version of Peter Rabbit 1893-1993.

AMIABLE GUINEA PIG™

Modeller: Albert Hallam
Height: 3 1/2", 8.9 cm
Colour: Tan jacket, white waistcoat, yellow trousers
Issued: 1967 - 1983

BEATRIX POTTER'S
"Amiable Guinea-Pig"
F. Warne & Co.Ltd.
Copyright
BESWICK ENGLAND

Back Stamp	*Beswick Number*	*Doulton Number*	*U.S. $*	*Price Can. $*	*U.K. £*	*Aust. $*
BP-2	2061	P2061	800.00	900.00	375.00	950.00
BP-3			500.00	690.00	275.00	700.00

AND THIS PIG HAD NONE™

Modeller: Martyn Alcock
Height: 4 ′, 10.1 cm
Colour: Mauve dress, mottled burgundy and green shawl, brown hat
Issued: 1992 to the present

ROYAL ALBERT ®
ENGLAND
And this Pig had none
Beatrix Potter
© F. WARNE & CO. 1992
© 1992 ROYAL ALBERT LTD

Back Stamp	*Beswick Number*	*Doulton Number*	*U.S. $*	*Price Can. $*	*U.K. £*	*Aust. $*
BP-6	3319	P3319	29.95	49.95	13.50	57.00

ANNA MARIA™

Modeller: Albert Hallam
Height: 3", 7.6 cm
Colour: Pale blue dress and white apron
Issued: 1963 - 1983

BEATRIX POTTER'S
Anna Maria
F. WARNE & CO. LTD
COPYRIGHT
BESWICK
ENGLAND

Back Stamp	*Beswick Number*	*Doulton Number*	*U.S. $*	*Price Can. $*	*U.K. £*	*Aust. $*
BP-2	1851	P1851	525.00	550.00	250.00	600.00
BP-3			275.00	375.00	175.00	400.00

APPLEY DAPPLY™
First Version (Bottle out)

Modeller: Albert Hallam
Height: 3 1/4", 8.3 cm
Colour: Brown mouse, white apron blue trim. Blue bow. Yellow basket, tray of jam tarts
Issued: 1971 to 1973

BEATRIX POTTER'S
APPLEY DAPPLY
F. WARNE & CO. LTD
COPYRIGHT
BESW
ENGLAND

Back Stamp	*Beswick Number*	*Doulton Number*	*U.S. $*	*Price Can. $*	*U.K. £*	*Aust. $*
BP-2	2333	P2333/1	1,000.00	1,000.00	500.00	1,000.00
BP-3			400.00	500.00	250.00	600.00

APPLEY DAPPLY™
Second Version (Bottle in)

Modeller: Albert Hallam
Height: 3 1/4", 8.3 cm
Colour: Brown mouse, white apron blue trim. Blue bow. Yellow basket, tray of jam tarts
Issued: 1973 to the present

BEATRIX POTTER'S
APPLEY DAPPLY
F Warne & Co.Ltd
c Copyright 1971
BESWICK
ENGLAND

Back Stamp	*Beswick Number*	*Doulton Number*	*U.S. $*	*Price Can. $*	*U.K. £*	*Aust. $*
BP-3	2333	P2333/2	75.00	100.00	45.00	100.00
BP-4			85.00	115.00	45.00	125.00
BP-6			29.95	47.00	13.50	57.00

AUNT PETTITOES™

Modeller: Albert Hallam
Height: 3 3/4", 9.5 cm
Colour: Blue dress and white cap with blue polka dots
Issued: 1970 - 1993

BEATRIX POTTER'S
"Aunt Pettitoes"
F. Warne & Co.Ltd.
© Copyright 1970
BESWICK
ENGLAND

Back Stamp	*Beswick Number*	*Doulton Number*	*U.S. $*	*Price Can. $*	*U.K. £*	*Aust.*
BP-2	2276	P2276	700.00	800.00	400.00	900.00
BP-3			75.00	90.00	50.00	100.00
BP-4			85.00	115.00	50.00	125.00
BP-6			45.00	50.00	20.00	75.00

BABBITTY BUMBLE™

Modeller: Warren Platt
Height: 2 3/4", 7.0 cm
Colour: Black and gold
Issued: 1989 - 1993

Back Stamp	Beswick Number	Doulton Number	Price U.S. $	Can. $	U.K. £	Aust. $
BP-6	2971	P2971	55.00	70.00	30.00	70.00

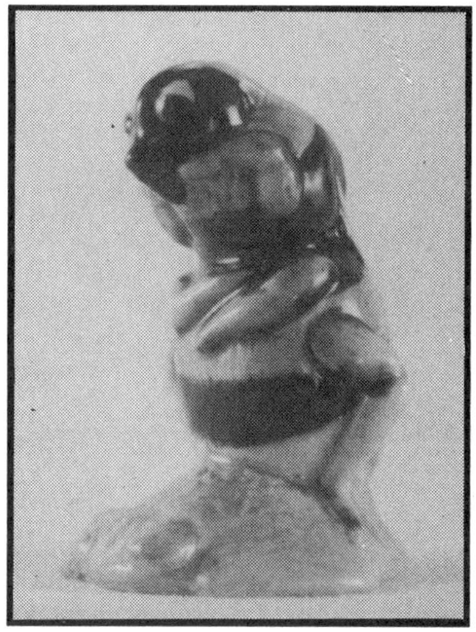

BENJAMIN ATE A LETTUCE LEAF™

Modeller: Martyn Alcock
Height: 4 3/4", 11.9 cm
Colour: Brown and white and yellow
Issued: 1992 to the present

Back Stamp	Beswick Number	Doulton Number	Price U.S. $	Can. $	U.K. £	Aust. $
BP-6	3317	P3317	29.95	49.95	13.50	65.00

BENJAMIN BUNNY™
First Version (Ears out, Shoes out)

Modeller: Arthur Gredington
Height: 4", 10.1 cm
Colour: Variation No. 1 — Pale green jacket
Variation No. 2 — Brown jaacket
Issued: 1948 - 1974

Back Stamp	Colour Variation	U.S. $	Can. $	Price U.K. £	Aust. $
BP-1		600.00	600.00	300.00	550.00
BP-2	Pale green jacket	550.00	550.00	275.00	500.00
BP-2	Brown jacket	550.00	550.00	275.00	500.00
BP-3		425.00	500.00	200.00	325.00

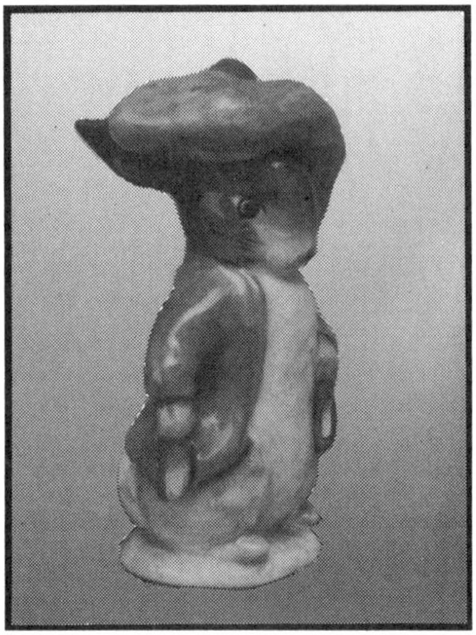

BENJAMIN BUNNY™
Second Version (Ears out, Shoes in)

Modeller:	Arthur Gredington
Height:	4", 10.1 cm
Colour:	Variation No. 1 — Pale green jacket Variation No. 2 — Brown jacket
Issued:	1972 - c.1980

Back Stamp	*Colour Variation*	*U.S. $*	*Price Can. $*	*U.K. £*	*Aust. $*
BP-2		500.00	500.00	300.00	550.00
BP-3	Pale green jacket	250.00	325.00	250.00	325.00
BP-3	Brown jacket	250.00	325.00	250.00	325.00

BENJAMIN BUNNY™
Third Version (Ears in, Shoes in)

Modeller:	Arthur Gredington
Height:	4", 10.1 cm
Colour:	Tan jacket, green beret with orange pom-pom
Issued:	c.1980 to the present

Back Stamp	*Beswick Number*	*Doulton Number*	*U.S. $*	*Price Can. $*	*U.K. £*	*Aust. $*
BP-3	1105/3	P1105/3	60.00	75.00	65.00	100.00
BP-4			65.00	85.00	65.00	90.00
BP-5			125.00	150.00	85.00	175.00
BP-6			29.95	47.00	13.50	57.00

BENJAMIN BUNNY™
Fourth Version (Large)

Modeller:	Martyn Alcock
Height:	6 1/4", 15.9 cm
Colour:	Tan jacket, Green beret with orange pom-pom
Issued:	1994 to the present

Back Stamp	*Beswick Number*	*Doulton Number*	*U.S. $*	*Price Can. $*	*U.K.£*	*Aust. $*
BP-6	3403	P3403	65.00	91.00	27.00	125.00

BENJAMIN BUNNY SAT ON A BANK™
First Version - Head looks down

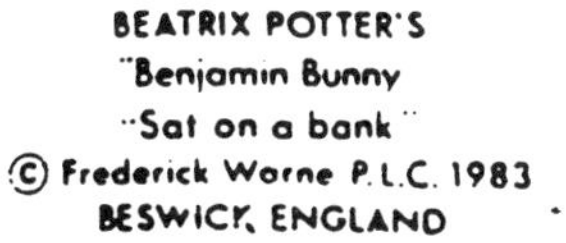

Modeller: David Lyttleton
Height: 3 3/4", 9.5 cm
Colour: Brown jacket
Issued: 1983 - 1988

Back Stamp	*Beswick Number*	*Doulton Number*	*U.S. $*	*Price Can. $*	*U.K. £*	*Aust. $*
BP-3	2803/1	P2803/1	125.00	150.00	95.00	165.00

BENJAMIN BUNNY SAT ON A BANK™
Second Version - Head looks up

Modeller: David Lyttleton
Height: 3 3/4", 9.5 cm
Colour: Golden brown jacket
Issued: 1988 to the present

Back Stamp	*Beswick Number*	*Doulton Number*	*U.S. $*	*Price Can. $*	*U.K. £*	*Aust. $*
BP-3	2803/2	P2803/2	150.00	175.00	110.00	190.00
BP-4			75.00	100.00	50.00	100.00
BP-6			29.95	49.95	13.50	57.00

BENJAMIN WAKES UP™

Modeller: Amanda Hughes-Lubeck
Height: 2 1/4", 5.7 cm
Colour: Green, white and orange
Issued: 1991 to the present

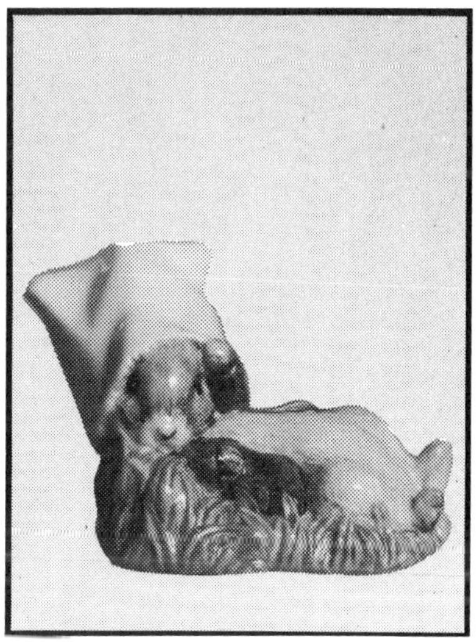

Back Stamp	*Beswick Number*	*Doulton Number*	*U.S. $*	*Price Can. $*	*U.K. £*	*Aust. $*
BP-6	3234	P3234	29.95	49.95	13.50	65.00

CECILY PARSLEY™
First Version (Deep Light Blue Dress, Head Down)

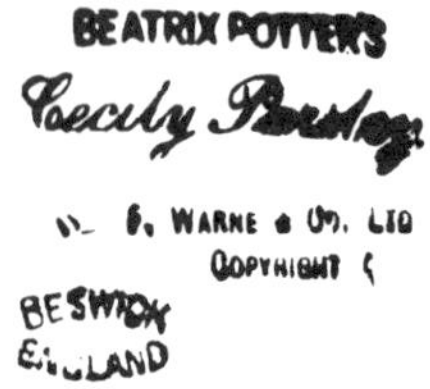

Modeller: Arthur Gredington
Height: 4", 10.1 cm
Colour: Deep light blue dress, white apron, brown pail
Issued: 1965 - 1985

Back Stamp	*Beswick Number*	*Doulton Number*	*U.S. $*	*Price Can. $*	*U.K. £*	*Aust. $*
BP-2	1941/1	P1941/1	325.00	175.00	75.00	175.00
BP-3			85.00	100.00	45.00	100.00

CECILY PARSLEY™
Second Version (Pale Light Blue Dress, Head Up)

Modeller: Arthur Gredington
Height: 4", 10.1 cm
Colour: Pale light blue dress, white apron
Issued: 1985 - 1993

Back Stamp	*Beswick Number*	*Doulton Number*	*U.S. $*	*Price Can. $*	*U.K. £*	*Aust. $*
BP-3	1941/2	P1941/2	75.00	100.00	45.00	100.00
BP-4			75.00	100.00	45.00	85.00
BP-6			30.00	50.00	25.00	65.00

CHIPPY HACKEE™

Modeller: David Lyttleton
Height: 3 3/4"
Colour: Pale green blanket, white handkerchief, green foot bath
Issued: 1979 - 1993

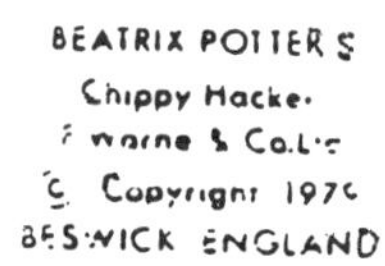

Back Stamp	*Beswick Number*	*Doulton Number*	*U.S. $*	*Price Can. $*	*U.K. £*	*Aust. $*
BP-3	2627	P2627	85.00	115.00	50.00	120.00
BP-4			100.00	150.00	50.00	150.00
BP-6			40.00	40.00	20.00	57.00

CHRISTMAS STOCKING™

Modeller:	Martyn Alcock
Height:	3 1/4", 8.3 cm
Colour:	Brown mice, red and white striped stocking
Issued:	1991 - 1994

ROYAL ALBERT ®
ENGLAND
The Christmas Stocking
Beatrix Potter
© F. WARNE & CO. 1991
© 1991 ROYAL ALBERT LTD

Back Stamp	*Beswick Number*	*Doulton Number*	*U.S. $*	*Price Can. $*	*U.K. £*	*Aust. $*
BP-6	3257	P3257	125.00	150.00	30.00	75.00

COTTONTAIL™

Modeller:	David Lyttleton
Height:	3 3/4", 9.5 cm
Colour:	Blue dress, brown chair
Issued:	1985 to the present

ROYAL ALBERT
Cottontail

Back Stamp	*Beswick Number*	*Doulton Number*	*U.S. $*	*Price Can. $*	*U.K.£*	*Aust. $*
BP-3	2878	P2878	60.00	75.00	40.00	75.00
BP-4			75.00	100.00	40.00	100.00
BP-6			29.95	54.00	13.50	55.00

COUSIN RIBBY™

Modeller:	Albert Hallam
Height:	3 1/2", 8.9 cm
Colour:	Pink skirt and hat, green apron, blue shawl, yellow basket
Issued:	1970 - 1993

BEATRIX POTTER'S
"Cousin Ribby"
F. Warne & Co.Ltd.
© Copyright 1970
BESWICK ENGLAND

Back Stamp	*Beswick Number*	*Doulton Number*	*U.S. $*	*Price Can. $*	*U.K. £*	*Aust. $*
BP-2	2284	P2284	250.00	300.00	125.00	325.00
BP-3			65.00	90.00	45.00	90.00
BP-4			75.00	100.00	35.00	100.00
BP-6			30.00	50.00	20.00	60.00

DIGGORY DIGGORY DELVET™

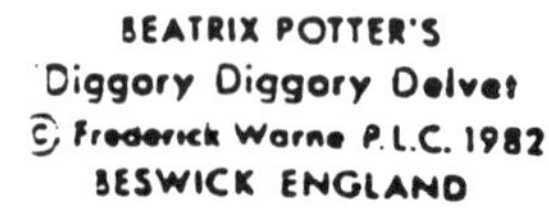

Modeller: David Lyttleton
Height: 2 3/4", 7 cm
Colour: Grey mole
Issued: 1982 to the present

Back Stamp	*Beswick Number*	*Doulton Number*	*U.S. $*	*Price Can. $*	*U.K. £*	*Aust. $*
BP-3	2713	P2713	70.00	100.00	45.00	150.00
BP-4			85.00	125.00	50.00	135.00
BP-6			29.95	49.95	13.50	70.00

DISPLAY STAND™

Modeller: Andrew Brindley
Height: 12 1/2" x 12 1/2", 31.7 cm x 31.7 cm
Colour: Brown, light brown
Issued: 1970 to the present

Back Stamp	*Beswick Number*	*Doulton Number*	*U.S. $*	*Price Can. $*	*U.K. £*	*Aust. $*
Beswick	2295	P2295	150.00	200.00	60.00	200.00
Doulton			150.00	175.00	35.00	90.00

DUCHESS™
Style One (Holding Flowers)

Modeller: Graham Orwell
Height: 3 3/4", 9.5 cm
Colour: Black dog holding bunch of flowers
Issued: 1955 - 1967

Back Stamp	*Beswick Number*	*Doulton Number*	*U.S. $*	*Price Can. $*	*U.K. £*	*Aust. $*
BP-2	1355	P1355	*2,500.00*	*3,000.00*	*1,500.00*	*3,000.00*

Note: The above italized prices for this rare figure are indications only, and the actual selling price may be higher or lower, depending on market conditions.

DUCHESS™
Style Two (Holding a Pie)

Modeller:	Graham Tongue
Height:	4", 10.1 cm
Colour:	Black dog, blue bow, light brown pie
Issued:	1979-1982

Back Stamp	*Beswick Number*	*Doulton Number*	*U.S. $*	*Price Can. $*	*U.K. £*	*Aust. $*
BP-3	2601	P2601	225.00	300.00	175.00	300.00

FIERCE BAD RABBIT™
First Version (Feet out)

Modeller:	David Lyttleton
Height:	4 3/4", 12.1 cm
Colour:	Brown and white rabbit, red-brown carrot, green seat
Issued:	1977 to 1980

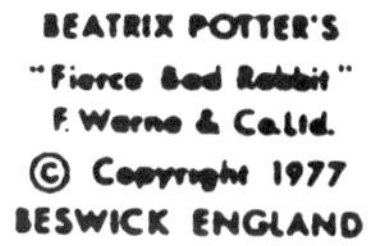

Back Stamp	*Beswick Number*	*Doulton Number*	*U.S. $*	*Price Can. $*	*U.K. £*	*Aust. $*
BP-3	2586	P2586/1	225.00	350.00	145.00	350.00

FIERCE BAD RABBIT™
Second Version (Feet in)

Modeller:	David Lyttleton
Height:	4 3/4", 12.1 cm
Colour:	Brown and white rabbit, red-brown carrot, green seat
Issued:	1980 to the present

Back Stamp	*Beswick Number*	*Doulton Number*	*U.S. $*	*Price Can. $*	*U.K. £*	*Aust. $*
BP-3	2586	P2586	70.00	100.00	45.00	125.00
BP-4			75.00	125.00	45.00	125.00
BP-6			29.95	47.00	13.50	70.00

FLOPSY, MOPSY AND COTTONTAIL™

Modeller: Arthur Gredington
Height: 2 1/2", 6.4 cm
Colour: Brown and white rabbits wearing rose-pink cloaks
Issued: 1954 to the present

BEATRIX POTTER'S
Flopsy Mopsy and Cottontail"
F. Warne & Co.Ltd.
C. Copyright 1954
BESWICK ENGLAND

Back Stamp	*Beswick Number*	*Doulton Number*	*U.S. $*	*Price Can. $*	*U.K. £*	*Aust. $*
BP-1	1274	P1274	400.00	450.00	200.00	500.00
BP-2			350.00	375.00	125.00	425.00
BP-3			70.00	80.00	45.00	80.00
BP-4			75.00	90.00	40.00	90.00
BP-5			125.00	150.00	85.00	175.00
BP-6			29.95	47.00	13.50	60.00

FOXY READING COUNTRY NEWS™

Modeller: Amanda Hughes-Lubeck
Height: 4 1/4", 10.8 cm
Colour: Brown and green
Issued: 1990 to the present

ROYAL ALBERT ®
ENGLAND
Foxy Reading
Beatrix Potter
© F. WARNE & CO. 1990
© 1990 ROYAL ALBERT LTD

Back Stamp	*Beswick Number*	*Doulton Number*	*U.S. $*	*Price Can. $*	*U.K. £*	*Aust. $*
BP-6	3219	P3219	49.95	69.50	21.00	110.00

FOXY WHISKERED GENTLEMAN™
First Version (Head Right)

Modeller: Arthur Gredington
Height: 4 3/4", 12.1 cm
Colour: Pale green jacket and trousers, pink waistcoat
Issued: 1954 to the present

BEATRIX POTTER'S
Foxy Whiskered Gentleman
BESWICK
ENGLAND
F. WARNE & CO. LTD.
COPYRIGHT

Back Stamp	*Beswick Number*	*Doulton Number*	*U.S. $*	*Price Can. $*	*U.K. £*	*Aust. $*
BP-1	1277	P1277	400.00	450.00	250.00	500.00
BP-2			300.00	350.00	250.00	500.00
BP-3			65.00	125.00	60.00	125.00
BP-4			75.00	125.00	60.00	140.00
BP-6			29.95	47.00	13.50	57.00

FOXY WHISKERED GENTLEMAN™
Third Version (Large size)

Modeller: Arthur Gredington
Height: 6", 15 cm
Colour: Pale green jacket and trousers, pink waistcoat
Issued: 1995 to the present

ROYAL ALBERT ®
ENGLAND
Foxy Whiskered
Gentleman
Beatrix Potter
© F. WARNE & CO.1994
© 1994 ROYAL ALBERT LTD.

Back Stamp	*Beswick Number*	*Doulton Number*	*U.S. $*	*Price Can. $*	*U.K. £*	*Aust. $*
BP-6	3450	P3450	65.00	91.00	27.00	125.00

GENTLEMAN MOUSE MADE A BOW™

Modeller: Ted Chawner
Height: 3", 7.6 cm
Colour: Brown, blue and white
Issued: 1990 to the present

ROYAL ALBERT ®
ENGLAND
Gentleman Mouse
Made a Bow
Beatrix Potter
© F. WARNE & CO. 1989
© 1989 ROYAL ALBERT LTD

Back Stamp	*Beswick Number*	*Doulton Number*	*U.S. $*	*Price Can. $*	*U.K. £*	*Aust. $*
BP-6	3200	P3200	29.95	49.95	13.50	70.00

GINGER™

Modeller: David Lyttleton
Height: 3 3/4", 9.5 cm
Colour: Green, white and brown
Issued: 1976 - 1982

BEATRIX POTTER'S
"Ginger"
F. Warne & Co.Ltd.
© Copyright 1976
BESWICK ENGLAND

Back Stamp	*Beswick Number*	*Doulton Number*	*U.S. $*	*Price Can. $*	*U.K. £*	*Aust. $*
BP-3	2559	P2559	900.00	1,100.00	500.00	700.00

GOODY TIPTOES™

Modeller: Arthur Gredington
Height: 3 1/2", 8.9 cm
Colour: Grey squirrel wearing pink dress and white apron, brown sack with yellow nuts
Issued: 1961 to the present

BEATRIX POTTER'S
"Goody Tiptoes"
F. Warne & Co.Ltd.
© Copyright 1961
BESWICK
ENGLAND

Back Stamp	*Beswick Number*	*Doulton Number*	*U.S. $*	*Price Can. $*	*U.K. £*	*Aust. $*
BP-2	1675	P1675	275.00	300.00	95.00	350.00
BP-3			65.00	80.00	40.00	90.00
BP-4			75.00	95.00	45.00	110.00
BP-6			29.95	47.00	13.50	64.00

Note: Goody Tiptoes was issued with two different bases.

GOODY AND TIMMY TIPTOES™

Modeller: David Lyttleton
Height: 4", 10.1 cm
Colour: Timmy: Rose coat
Goody: Pink overdress with green and biege underskirt, green umbrella
Issued: 1986 to the present

ROYAL ALBERT ®
ENGLAND
Goody and Timmy Tiptoes
Beatrix Potter
© F WARNE & CO 1986
© 1989 ROYAL ALBERT LTD

Back Stamp	*Beswick Number*	*Doulton Number*	*U.S. $*	*Price Can. $*	*U.K. £*	*Aust. $*
BP-3	2957	P2957	275.00	300.00	150.00	300.00
BP-4			325.00	375.00	150.00	350.00
BP-6			49.95	88.00	24.00	85.00

HUNCA MUNCA™

Modeller: Arthur Gredington
Height: 2 3/4", 7 cm
Colour: Blue dress, white apron, pink blanket and straw cradle
Issued: 1951 to the present

BESWICK ENGLAND
BEATRIX POTTER'S
"HUNCA MUNCA"
F. WARNE & CO. LTD.
COPYRIGHT

Back Stamp	*Beswick Number*	*Doulton Number*	*U.S. $*	*Price Can. $*	*U.K. £*	*Aust. $*
BP-1	1198	P1198	295.00	350.00	125.00	350.00
BP-2			250.00	300.00	100.00	325.00
BP-3			65.00	100.00	65.00	110.00
BP-4			75.00	125.00	60.00	135.00
BP-5			125.00	150.00	85.00	150.00
BP-6			29.95	47.00	13.50	57.00

HUNCA MUNCA SPILLS THE BEADS™

ROYAL ALBERT ®
ENGLAND
Hunca Munca
spills the beads
Beatrix Potter
© F WARNE & CO 1991
© 1992 ROYAL ALBERT LTD

Modeller:	Martyn Alcock
Height:	3 1/4", 8.3 cm
Colour:	Brown mouse, blue and white rice jar
Issued:	1992 to the present

Back Stamp	*Beswick Number*	*Doulton Number*	*U.S. $*	*Price Can. $*	*U.K. £*	*Aust. $*
BP-6	3288	P3288	29.95	49.95	15.95	70.00

HUNCA MUNCA SWEEPING™

BEATRIX POTTER'S
Hunca Munca Sweeping
F Warne & Co Ltd.
© Copyright 1977
BESWICK ENGLAND

Modeller:	David Lyttleton
Height:	3 1/2", 8.9 cm
Colour:	Mauve patterned dress with white apron, green broom handle
Issued:	1977 to the present

Back Stamp	*Beswick Number*	*Doulton Number*	*U.S. $*	*Price Can. $*	*U.K. £*	*Aust. $*
BP-3	2584	P2584	65.00	130.00	65.00	175.00
BP-4			75.00	150.00	75.00	175.00
BP-6			29.95	47.00	13.50	57.00

BEATRIX POTTER'S
Jemima Puddleduck
F. Warne & Co. Ltd
Copyright
BESWICK
ENGLAND

JEMIMA PUDDLE-DUCK™

First Version

Modeller:	Arthur Gredington
Height:	4 3/4", 12.1cm
Colour:	White duck, mauve shawl, light blue bonnet
Issued:	1948 to the present

Back Stamp	*Beswick Number*	*Doulton Number*	*U.S. $*	*Price Can. $*	*U.K. £*	*Aust. $*
BP-1	1092/1	P1092/1	275.00	325.00	125.00	350.00
BP-2			225.00	250.00	100.00	300.00
BP-3			65.00	90.00	65.00	100.00
BP-4			75.00	100.00	45.00	115.00
BP-5			125.00	150.00	85.00	175.00
BP-6			29.95	47.00	13.50	64.00

Note: Jemima Puddle-duck was issued with two different bases.

JEMIMA PUDDLE-DUCK™
Second Version (Large size)

Modeller: Arthur Gredington
Height: 6", 15 cm
Colour: White duck, mauve shawl light blue bonnet
Issued: 1993 to the present

Beswick Ware
MADE IN ENGLAND
BEATRIX POTTER'S
JEMIMA PUDDLE-DUCK
BESWICK CENTENARY
1894 - 1994
© F. WARNE & CO. 1993
© 1993 ROYAL DOULTON

Back Stamp	Beswick Number	Doulton Number	U.S. $	Price Can. $	U.K. £	Aust. $
BP-6	1092/2	P1092/2	65.00	91.00	35.00	125.00
BP-7			65.00	88.00	27.00	98.00

JEMIMA PUDDLE-DUCK CHARACTER JUG™

Modeller: Ted Chawner
Height: 4", 10.1 cm
Colour: Blue, pink and white
Issued: 1989 - 1992

BEATRIX POTTER
'Jemima Puddle-Duck'
© F. Warne & Co. 1988
Licensed by Copyrights
John Beswick
Studio of Royal Doulton
England

Back Stamp	Beswick Number	Doulton Number	U.S. $	Price Can. $	U.K. £	Aust. $
BP-4	3088	P3088	150.00	225.00	75.00	100.00
BP-6			115.00	135.00	50.00	90.00

JEMIMA PUDDLE-DUCK AND FOXY WHISKERED GENTLEMAN™

Modeller: Ted Chawner
Height: 4 3/4", 12.1 cm
Colour: Brown, green, white and blue
Issued: 1990 to the present

ROYAL ALBERT ®
ENGLAND
Jemima Puddleduck with
Foxy Whiskered Gentleman
Beatrix Potter
© F WARNE & CO 1989
© 1989 ROYAL ALBERT LTD

Back Stamp	Beswick Number	Doulton Number	U.S. $	Price Can. $	U.K. £	Aust. $
BP-6	3193	P3193	49.95	100.00	24.95	100.00

JEMIMA PUDDLE-DUCK™
Large Size Wall Plaque Gold Backstamp Character Jug

DISPLAY STAND
Pig-Wig™ Simpkin™ Duchess™ Ginger™ Amiable Guinea Pig™

TIMMY TIPTOES™
First Version Second Version

SQUIRREL NUTKIN™
First Version Second Version

TOM KITTEN™
First Version Second Version

PETER RABBIT™
First Version Second Version

APPLEY DAPPLY™ MRS. TIGGY WINKLE™

First Version Second Version First Version Second Version on a Tree Lamp Base

TOMMY BROCK™ MR. BENJAMIN BUNNY™

Spade Out Spade In First Version Second Version

MISS MOPPET™
First Version Second Version

TABITHA TWITCHIT™
First Version Second Version

LITTLE PIG ROBINSON™
First Version Second Version

PIGLING BLAND™
First Version Second Version

FIERCE BAD RABBIT™
First Version Second Version

BENJAMIN BUNNY SAT ON A BANK™
First Version Second Version

MR. JEREMY FISHER™
First Version Second Version

MR. JACKSON™
First Version Second Version

BENJAMIN BUNNY™
First Version Second Version Third Version

MRS. RABBIT™
First Version Second Version

CECILEY PARSLEY™
First Version Second Version

TOM KITTEN™

Character Jug | Large Size | First Version | Second Version

PETER RABBIT™

Large Size | First Version | Second Version | Character Jug

TOMMY BROCK™
First Version Second Version Third Version Fourth Version

DUCHESS™
Style Two Style One

JEMIMA PUDDLE-DUCK AND FOXY WHISKERED GENTLEMAN PLAQUE™

Modeller: Harry Sales and David Lyttleton
Height: 7 1/2" x 7 1/2", 19.1 cm x 19.1 cm
Colour: Brown, green, white and blue
Issued: 1977 - 1982

Back Stamp	*Beswick Number*	*Doulton Number*	*U.S. $*	*Price Can. $*	*U.K. £*	*Aust. S*
BP-3	2594	P2594	175.00	200.00	95.00	235.00

JEMIMA PUDDLEDUCK MADE A FEATHER NEST™

Modeller: David Lyttleton
Height: 2 1/4", 5.7 cm
Colour: Blue hat, mauve and green shawl and white duck
Issued: 1983 to the present

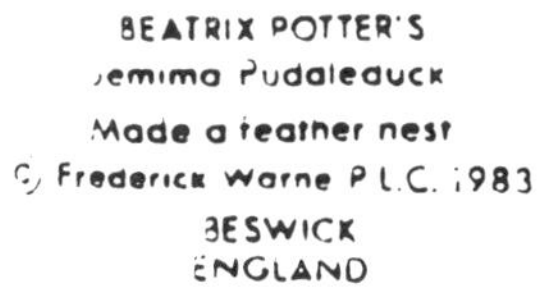

Back Stamp	*B M*	*Doulton Number*	*U.S. $*	*Price Can. $*	*U.K. £*	*Aust. $*
BP-3	2823	P2823	65.00	80.00	40.00	100.00
BP-4			75.00	100.00	40.00	115.00
BP-6			29.95	0.00	13.50	57.00

JEMIMA PUDDLE-DUCK PLAQUE™

Modeller: Albert Hallam
Height: 6", 15.2 cm
Colour: White duck, mauve shawl
Issued: 1967 - 1969

Back Stamp	*Beswick Number*	*Doulton Number*	*U.S. $*	*Price Can. $*	*U.K. £*	*Aust. $*
BP-2	2082	P2082		Extremely Rare		

Photograph not available at press time

JOHN JOINER™

Modeller:	Graham Tongue
Height:	2 1/2", 6.4 cm
Colour:	Brown dog wearing green jacket
Issued:	1990 to the present

ROYAL ALBERT ®
ENGLAND
John Joiner
Beatrix Potter
© F. WARNE & CO. 1990
© 1990 ROYAL ALBERT LTD

Back Stamp	*Beswick Number*	*Doulton Number*	*U.S. $*	*Price Can. $*	*U.K. £*	*Aust. $*
BP-6	2965	P2965	29.95	49.95	13.50	75.00

JOHNNY TOWN-MOUSE™

Modeller:	Arthur Gredington
Height:	3 1/2", 8.9 cm
Colour:	Pale blue jacket, white and brown waistcoat
Issued:	1954 - 1993

BEATRIX POTTER'S
"Johnny Town-Mouse"
F. Warne & Co.Ltd.
© Copyright 1954
BESWICK ENGLAND

Back Stamp	*Beswick Number*	*Doulton Number*	*U.S. $*	*Price Can. $*	*U.K. £*	*Aust. $*
BP-1	1276	P1276	275.00	350.00	125.00	400.00
BP-2			225.00	250.00	95.00	275.00
BP-3			65.00	90.00	45.00	110.00
BP-4			75.00	100.00	45.00	125.00
BP-6			30.00	50.00	20.00	57.00

JOHNNY TOWN-MOUSE WITH BAG™

Modeller:	Ted Chawner
Height:	3 1/2", 8.9 cm
Colour:	Light brown coat and hat, yellow/cream waistcoat
Issued:	1988 - 1994

BEATRIX POTTER
"Johnny Town-Mouse with Bag"
© Frederick Warne & Co. 1988
Licensed by Copyrights
Studio of Royal Doulton
England

Back Stamp	*Beswick Number*	*Doulton Number*	*U.S. $*	*Price Can. $*	*U.K. £*	*Aust. $*
BP-4	3094	P3094	250.00	375.00	175.00	400.00
BP-6			100.00	115.00	30.00	70.00

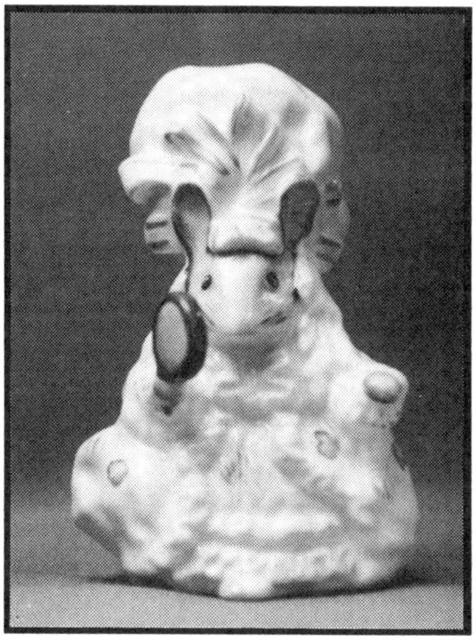

LADY MOUSE™

Modeller: Arthur Gredington
Height: 4", 10.1 cm
Colour: White dress with yellow trim and blue polka dot sleeves, white hat with purple and blue highlights
Issued: 1950 to the present

Back Stamp	Beswick Number	Doulton Number	U.S. $	Price Can. $	U.K. £	Aust. $
BP-1	1183	P1183	325.00	375.00	150.00	400.00
BP-2			275.00	300.00	110.00	350.00
BP-3			75.00	180.00	55.00	125.00
BP-4			85.00	125.00	55.00	140.00
BP-6			29.95	49.95	13.50	64.00

LADY MOUSE MADE A CURTSEY™

Modeller: Amanda Hughes-Lubeck
Height: 3 1/4", 8.3 cm
Colour: Purple-pink and white
Issued: 1990 to the present

Back Stamp	Beswick Number	Doulton Number	U.S. $	Price Can. $	U.K. £	Aust. $
BP-6	3220	P3220	29.95	49.95	13.50	75.00

LITTLE BLACK RABBIT™

Modeller: David Lyttleton
Height: 4 1/2", 11.4 cm
Colour: Black rabbit wearing green waistcoat
Issued: 1977 to the present

Back Stamp	Beswick Number	Doulton Number	U.S. $	Price Can. $	U.K. £	Aust. $
BP-3	2585	P2585	65.00	90.00	50.00	125.00
BP-4			75.00	115.00	50.00	125.00
BP-6			29.95	47.00	13.50	85.00

LITTLE PIG ROBINSON™
First Version (Blue Stripes)

Modeller: Arthur Gredington
Height: 4", 10.2 cm
Colour: White and blue striped dress; brown basket with yellow cauliflowers
Issued: 1948 - 1974

BEATRIX POTTER'S
Little Pig Robinson
F. WARNE & Co. LTD.
COPYRIGHT
BESWICK
ENGLAND

Back Stamp	*Beswick Number*	*Doulton Number*	*U.S. $*	*Price Can. $*	*U.K. £*	*Aust. $*
BP-1	1104/1	P1104/1	600.00	650.00	275.00	700.00
BP-2			500.00	550.00	225.00	500.00
BP-3			500.00	550.00	225.00	500.00

LITTLE PIG ROBINSON™
Second Version (Blue Checked)

Modeller: Arthur Gredington
Height: 3 1/2", 8.9 cm
Colour: Blue dress, brown basket with cream cauliflowers
Issued: c.1970 to the present

BEATRIX POTTER'S
"Little Pig Robinson"
F. Warne & Co.Ltd.
© Copyright 1948
BESWICK
ENGLAND

Back Stamp	*Beswick Number*	*Doulton Number*	*U.S. $*	*Price Can. $*	*U.K. £*	*Aust. $*
BP-2	1104/2	P1104/2		Extremely Rare		
BP-3			75.00	110.00	45.00	115.00
BP-4			85.00	125.00	45.00	130.00
BP-6			29.95	49.95	13.50	67.00

LITTLE PIG ROBINSON SPYING™

Modeller: Ted Chawner
Height: 3 1/2", 8.9 cm
Colour: Blue and white striped dress, rose-pink chair
Issued: 1987 - 1993

BEATRIX POTTER
"Little Pig Robinson
Spying"
© Frederick Warne & Co. 1987
Licensed by Copyrights
BESWICK ENGLAND

Back Stamp	*Beswick Number*	*Doulton Number*	*U.S. $*	*Price Can. $*	*U.K. £*	*Aust. $*
BP-3	3031	P3031	250.00	350.00	175.00	350.00
BP-4			275.00	350.00	175.00	350.00
BP-6			100.00	100.00	35.00	90.00

MISS DORMOUSE™

ROYAL ALBERT ®
ENGLAND
Miss Dormouse
Beatrix Potter
© F. WARNE & CO. 1991
© 1991 ROYAL ALBERT LTD

Modeller: Martyn Alcock
Height: 4", 10.1 cm
Colour: Blue, white and pink
Issued: 1991 - 1995

Back Stamp	*Beswick Number*	*Doulton Number*	*U.S. $*	*Price Can. $*	*U.K. £*	*Aust. $*
BP-6	3251	P3251	49.95	95.00	19.95	75.00

MISS MOPPET™
First Version (Mottled Brown Cat)

Modeller: Arthur Gredington
Height: 3", 7.6 cm
Colour: Dark brown cat, blue checkered kerchief
Issued: 1954 - c.1978

BEATRIX POTTER'S
"Miss. Moppet
F. Warne & Co.Ltd.
© Copyright 1954
BESWICK ENGLAND

Back Stamp	*Beswick Number*	*Doulton Number*	*U.S. $*	*Price Can. $*	*U.K. £*	*Aust. $*
BP-1	1275	P1275A	250.00	325.00	125.00	350.00
BP-2			225.00	275.00	95.00	300.00
BP-3			200.00	250.00	80.00	275.00

Note: The base is too small to carry the circle Beswick England backstamp. It is flattened and the copyright date is carried in script.

MISS MOPPET™
Second Version (Brown Striped Cat)

Modeller: Arthur Gredington
Height: 3", 7.6 cm
Colour: Light brown cat, blue checkered kerchief
Issued: 1978 to the present

BEATRIX POTTER'S
"Miss. Moppet
F. Warne & Co.Ltd.
© Copyright 1954
BESWICK ENGLAND

Back Stamp	*Beswick Number*	*Doulton Number*	*U.S. $*	*Price Can. $*	*U.K. £*	*Aust. $*
BP-3	1275	P1275B	65.00	100.00	45.00	115.00
BP-4			75.00	115.00	45.00	115.00
BP-6			29.95	47.00	13.50	57.00

MITTENS AND MOPPET™

Modeller: Ted Chawner
Height: 3 3/4", 9.5 cm
Colour: Blue, brown and grey
Issued: 1990 - 1994

ROYAL ALBERT ®
ENGLAND
Mittens and Moppet
Beatrix Potter
© F. WARNE & CO. 1989
© 1989 ROYAL ALBERT LTD

Back Stamp	Beswick Number	Doulton Number	U.S. $	Price Can. $	U.K. £	Aust. $
BP-6	3197	P3197	50.00	75.00	30.00	75.00

MOTHER LADYBIRD™

Modeller: Warren Platt
Height: 2 1/2", 6 .4 cm
Colour: Red and black
Issued: 1989 to the present

ROYAL ALBERT ®
ENGLAND
Mother Ladybird
Beatrix Potter
© F. WARNE & CO. 1989
© 1989 ROYAL ALBERT LTD

Back Stamp	Beswick Number	Doulton Number	U.S. $	Price Can. $	U.K. £	Aust. $
BP-6	2966	P2966	29.95	55.00	13.50	65.00

MR. ALDERMAN PTOLEMY™

Modeller: Graham Tongue
Height: 3 1/2", 8.9 cm
Colour: Brown, grey and green
Issued: 1973 to the present

BEATRIX POTTER'S
"Mr. Alderman Ptolemy"
F. Warne & Co. Ltd.
© Copyright 1973
BESWICK
MADE IN ENGLAND

Back Stamp	Beswick Number	Doulton Number	U.S. $	Price Can. $	U.K. £	Aust. $
BP-3	2424	P2424	85.00	200.00	85.00	225.00
BP-4			95.00	200.00	85.00	225.00
BP-6			29.95	47.00	13.50	64.00

MR. BENJAMIN BUNNY™
First Version (Pipe Out)

Modeller: Arthur Gredington
Height: 4 1/4", 10.8 cm
Colour: Dark maroon jacket, yellow waistcoat;
Issued: 1965 - 1974

Back Stamp	*Beswick Number*	*Doulton Number*	*U.S. $*	*Price Can. $*	*U.K. £*	*Aust. $*
BP-2	1940/1	P1940/1	600.00	750.00	300.00	800.00
BP-3			500.00	650.00	275.00	700.00

MR. BENJAMIN BUNNY™
Second Version (Pipe In)

Modeller: Arthur Gredington
Height: 4 1/4", 10.8 cm
Colour: Variation No. 1 — Dark maroon jacket
Variation No. 2 — Lilac jacket
Issued: c.1970 - c.1972

BEATRIX POTTER'S
"Mr. Benjamin Bunny
F. Warne & Co.Ltd.
© Copyright 1965
BESWICK ENGLAND

Back Stamp	*Colour Variation*	*U.S. $*	*Price Can. $*	*U.K. £*	*Aust. $*
BP-3	Dark maroon jacket	500.00	650.00	275.00	700.00
BP-3	Lilac jacket	65.00	85.00	40.00	100.00
BP-4	Lilac jacket	75.00	85.00	40.00	100.00
BP-5	Lilac jacket	100.00	100.00	50.00	100.00
BP-6	Lilac jacket	29.95	47.00	13.50	62.00

MR. BENJAMIN BUNNY AND PETER RABBIT™

Modeller: Alan Maslankowski
Height: 4", 10.1 cm
Colour: Benjamin Bunny: Lilac jacket yellow waistcoat;
Peter Rabbit: blue jacket
Issued: 1975 - 1995

BEATRIX POTTER'S
Mr. Benjamin Bunny
& Peter Rabbit"
F. Warne & Co.Ltd.
© Copyright 1975
BESWICK ENGLAND

Back Stamp	*Beswick Number*	*Doulton Number*	*U.S. $*	*Price Can. $*	*U.K. £*	*Aust. $*
BP-3	2509	P2509	200.00	250.00	85.00	275.00
BP-4			225.00	275.00	95.00	300.00
BP-6			39.95	69.95	19.95	91.00

MR. DRAKE PUDDLE-DUCK™

Modeller: David Lyttleton
Height: 4", 10.1 cm
Colour: White duck, blue waistcoat and trousers
Issued: 1979 to the present

BEATRIX POTTER
"Mr. Drake Puddle-Duck"
© Frederick Warne & Co. 1979
Licensed by Copyrights
BESWICK ENGLAND

Back Stamp	*Beswick Number*	*Doulton Number*	*U.S. $*	*Price Can. $*	*U.K. £*	*Aust. $*
BP-3	2628	P2628	65.00	95.00	55.00	100.00
BP-4			75.00	110.00	65.00	115.00
BP-6			29.95	47.00	13.50	64.00

MR. JACKSON™
First Version (Green Frog)

Modeller: Albert Hallam
Height: 2 3/4", 7.0 cm
Colour: Green frog wearing mauve jacket
Issued: 1974 - c.1980

BEATRIX POTTER'S
"Mr Jackson"
F. Warne & Co.Ltd.
© Copyright 1974
BESWICK ENGLAND

Back Stamp	*Beswick Number*	*Doulton Number*	*U.S. $*	*Price Can. $*	*U.K. £*	*Aust. $*
BP-3	2453/1	P2453/1	550.00	625.00	250.00	550.00

MR. JACKSON™
Second Version (Brown Frog)

Modeller: Albert Hallam
Height: 2 3/4", 7.0 cm
Colour: Brown frog wearing mauve jacket
Issued: 1980 to the present

BEATRIX POTTER
Mr Jackson
F. Warne & Co.Ltd.
© Copyright 1974
BESWICK ENGLAND

Back Stamp	*Beswick Number*	*Doulton Number*	*U.S. $*	*Price Can. $*	*U.K. £*	*Aust. $*
BP-3	2453/2	P2453/2	65.00	130.00	65.00	140.00
BP-4			75.00	130.00	65.00	140.00
BP-6			29.95	47.00	13.50	70.00

MR. JEREMY FISHER™
First Version (Spotted Legs)

Modeller: Arthur Gredington
Height: 3", 7.6 cm
Colour: Lilac coat, green frog with small brown spots on head and legs
Issued: 1950 - c.1980

Back Stamp	*Beswick Number*	*Doulton Number*	*U.S. $*	*Price Can. $*	*U.K. £*	*Aust. $*
BP-1	1157/1	P1157/1	400.00	475.00	225.00	525.00
BP-2			325.00	350.00	160.00	375.00
BP-3			200.00	250.00	95.00	275.00

MR. JEREMY FISHER™
Second Version (Striped Legs)

Modeller: Arthur Gredington
Height: 3", 7.6 cm
Colour: Lilac coat, green frog with large spots on head and stripes on legs
Issued: c.1980 to the present

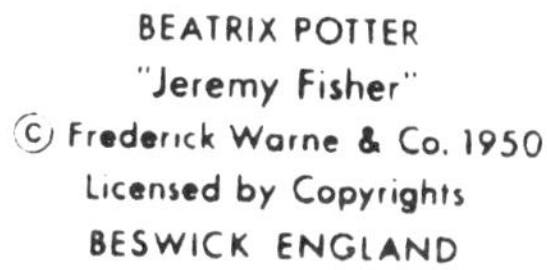

Back Stamp	*Beswick Number*	*Doulton Number*	*U.S. $*	*Price Can. $*	*U.K. £*	*Aust. $*
BP-3	1157/2	P1157/2	75.00	110.00	45.00	125.00
BP-4			85.00	125.00	45.00	140.00
BP-6			29.95	47.00	13.50	64.00

MR. JEREMY FISHER™
Third Version (Large size)

Modeller: Martyn Alcock
Height: 5", 12.7 cm
Size: Large
Colour: Lilac coat, green frog stripes on legs
Issued: 1994 to the present

Back Stamp	*Beswick Number*	*Doulton Number*	*U.S. $*	*Price Can. $*	*U.K. £*	*Aust. $*
BP-6	3372	P3372	65.00	91.00	27.00	125.00

MR. JEREMY FISHER CHARACTER JUG™

John Beswick
ENGLAND
BEATRIX POTTER
"Jeremy Fisher"
© 1987 Frederick Warne & Co.
Licensed by Copyrights

Modeller:	Graham Tongue
Height:	3", 7.6 cm
Colour:	Mauve
Issued:	1987 - 1992

Back Stamp	*Beswick Number*	*Doulton Number*	*U.S. $*	*Price Can. $*	*U.K. £*	*Aust. $*
BP-4	2960	P2960	135.00	150.00	65.00	125.00
BP-6			115.00	49.95	13.50	80.00

MR. JEREMY FISHER DIGGING™

BEATRIX POTTER
"Mr. Jeremy Fisher Digging"
© F. Warne & Co. 1988
Licensed by Copyrights
John Beswick
Studio of Royal Doulton
England

Modeller:	Ted Chawner
Height:	3 3/4", 9.5 cm
Colour:	Mauve coat, pink waistcoat, white cravat, green frog, with brown highlights
Issued:	1988 - 1994

Back Stamp	*Beswick Number*	*Doulton Number*	*U.S. $*	*Price Can. $*	*U.K. £*	*Aust. $*
BP-3	3090	P3090	250.00	350.00	150.00	400.00
BP-4			275.00	400.00	125.00	425.00
BP-6			50.00	75.00	35.00	70.00

MR. McGREGOR™

Modeller:	Martyn C. R. Alcock
Height:	5 1/4", 13.5cm
Colour:	Brown hat and trousers, tan vest and pale blue shirt
Issued:	1995 to the present

Back Stamp	*Beswick Number*	*Doulton Number*	*U.S. $*	*Price Can. $*	*U.K. £*	*Aust. $*
BP-6	3506	P3506	40.00	47.00	17.95	74.00

MR. TOD™

Modeller: Ted Chawner
Height: 4 3/4", 12.1 cm
Colour: Green suit, red waistcoat, dark brown walking stick
Issued: 1988 - 1993

Back Stamp	*Beswick Number*	*Doulton Number*	*U.S. $*	*Price Can. $*	*U.K. £*	*Aust. $*
BP-4	3091/1	P3091/1	275.00	400.00	175.00	350.00
BP-6			95.00	135.00	35.00	125.00

MRS. FLOPSY BUNNY™

Modeller: Arthur Gredington
Height: 4", 10.1 cm
Colour: Light blue dress, pink bag
Issued: 1965 to the present

Back Stamp	*Beswick Number*	*Doulton Number*	*U.S. $*	*Price Can. $*	*U.K. £*	*Aust. $*
BP-2	1942	P1942	225.00	225.00	95.00	250.00
BP-3			65.00	90.00	45.00	100.00
BP-4			75.00	115.00	45.00	125.00
BP-6			29.95	47.00	13.50	57.00

MRS RABBIT™

First Version (Umbrella Out)

Modeller: Arthur Gredington
Height: 4 1/4", 10.8 cm
Colour: Variation No. 1 — Pink and yellow striped dress
Variation No. 2 — Lilac and pale green striped dress
Issued: 1951 - c.1970

Back Stamp	*Beswick Number*	*Doulton Number*	*U.S. $*	*Price Can. $*	*U.K.£*	*Aust. $*
BP-2	Var. 1 — Pink/yellow		500.00	575.00	250.00	550.00
BP-2	Var. 2 — Lilac/pale green		500.00	575.00	250.00	550.00
BP-3			300.00	375.00	175.00	400.00

MRS RABBIT™
Second Version (Umbrella Moulded to Dress)

Modeller: Arthur Gredington
Height: 4 1/4", 10.8 cm
Colour: Rose-pink and yellow striped dress, red collar and cap, light straw coloured basket
Issued: c.1970 to the present

Back Stamp	*Beswick Number*	*Doulton Number*	*U.S. $*	*Price Can. $*	*U.K. £*	*Aust. $*
BP-3	1200/3	P1200/3	65.00	90.00	50.00	125.00
BP-4			75.00	100.00	50.00	125.00
BP-6			29.95	47.00	13.50	60.00

MRS RABBIT™
Third Version (Large Size)

Modeller: Martyn Alcock
Height: 6 1/4", 15.9 cm
Colour: White, pink, yellow and green
Issued: 1994 to the present

Back Stamp	*Beswick Number*	*Doulton Number*	*U.S. $*	*Price Can. $*	*U.K. £*	*Aust. $*
BP-6	3398	P3398	65.00	91.00	27.00	125.00

MRS. RABBIT AND BUNNIES™

Modeller: David Lyttleton
Height: 3 3/4", 9.5 cm
Colour: Blue dress with white apron; dark blue chair
Issued: 1976 to the present

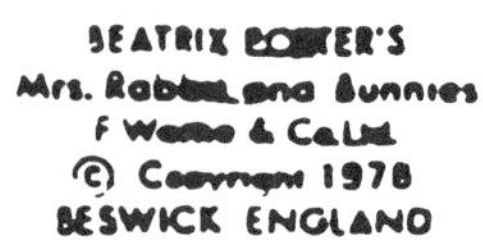

Back Stamp	*Beswick Number*	*Doulton Number*	*U.S. $*	*Price Can. $*	*U.K. £*	*Aust. $*
BP-3	2543	P2543	85.00	125.00	45.00	135.00
BP-4			95.00	140.00	50.00	150.00
BP-5			125.00	150.00	85.00	175.00
BP-6			29.95	47.00	13.50	60.00

MRS. RABBIT COOKING™

ROYAL ALBERT ®
ENGLAND
Mrs Rabbit cooking
Beatrix Potter
© F WARNE & CO 1991
© 1992 ROYAL ALBERT LTD

Modeller:	Martyn Alcock
Height:	4", 10.1 cm
Colour:	Blue dress, white apron
Issued:	1992 to the present

Back Stamp	*Beswick Number*	*Doulton Number*	*U.S. $*	*Price Can. $*	*U.K. £*	*Aust. $*
BP-6	3278	P3278	29.95	49.95	13.50	65.00

MRS TIGGY-WINKLE™
First Version (Diagonal Stripes)

BEATRIX POTTER'S
Mrs Tiggy-Winkle
Copyright
BESWICK ENGLAND

Modeller:	Arthur Gredington
Height:	3 1/4", 8.3 cm
Colour:	Red-brown and white dress, green and blue striped skirt, white apron
Issued:	1948 - 1974

Back Stamp	*Beswick Number*	*Doulton Number*	*U.S. $*	*Price Can.$*	*U.K. £*	*Aust. $*
BP-1	1107/1	P1107/1	300.00	400.00	125.00	450.00
BP-2			275.00	350.00	100.00	400.00
BP-3			150.00	200.00	75.00	175.00

MRS TIGGY-WINKLE™
Second Version (Square Stripes)

BEATRIX POTTER'S
"Mrs Tiggy Winkle"
F. Warne & Co.Ltd.
© Copyright 1948
BESWICK ENGLAND

Modeller:	Arthur Gredington
Height:	3 1/4", 8.3 cm
Colour:	Red-brown and white dress, green and blue striped skirt, white apron
Issued:	1972 to the present

Back Stamp	*Beswick Number*	*Doulton No.*	*U.S. $*	*Price Can. $*	*U.K. £*	*Aust. $*
BP-2	1107/2	P1107/2	275.00	350.00	100.00	400.00
BP-3			85.00	125.00	45.00	135.00
BP-4			95.00	135.00	45.00	150.00
BP-5			100.00	150.00	50.00	160.00
BP-6			29.95	47.00	13.50	60.00

MRS. TIGGY-WINKLE CHARACTER JUG™

Modeller: Ted Chawner
Height: 3", 7.6 cm
Colour: White dress with blue stripes
Issued: 1988 - 1992

Back Stamp	Beswick Number	Doulton Number	U.S. $	Price Can. $	U.K. £	Aust.
BP-4	3102	P3102	150.00	200.00	65.00	200.00
BP-6			115.00	150.00	50.00	150.00

MRS. TIGGY WINKLE TAKES TEA™

Modeller: David Lyttleton
Height: 3 1/4", 8.3 cm
Colour: Pink and white dress, white and brown mob cap
Issued: 1985 to the present

Back Stamp	Beswick Number	Doulton Number	U.S. $	Price Can. $	U.K. £	Aust. $
BP-3	2877	P2877	85.00	150.00	95.00	150.00
BP-4			95.00	175.00	110.00	175.00
BP-6			29.95	47.00	13.50	57.00

MRS TITTLEMOUSE™

Modeller: Arthur Gredington
Height: 3 1/2", 8.9 cm
Colour: White and red striped blouse; blue and white striped skirt
Issued: 1948 - 1993

Back Stamp	Beswick Number	Doulton Number	U.S. $	Price Can. $	U.K. £	Aust. $
BP-1	1103	P1103	300.00	450.00	110.00	450.00
BP-2			250.00	350.00	95.00	350.00
BP-3			65.00	100.00	60.00	110.00
BP-4			75.00	110.00	60.00	125.00
BP-6			35.00	50.00	25.00	60.00

MRS. TITTLEMOUSE PLAQUE™

Modeller: Harry Sales
Height: 7 1/2" x 7 1/2", 19.1 cm x 19.1 cm
Colour: Blue, pink and green
Issued: 1982 - 1984

Back Stamp	*Beswick Number*	*Doulton Number*	*U.S. $*	*Price Can. $*	*U.K. £*	*Aust. $*
BP-3	2685	P2685	150.00	200.00	95.00	150.00

NO MORE TWIST™

Modeller: Martyn Alcock
Height: 3 1/2", 9.2 cm
Colour: Brown and white mouse
Issued: 1992 to the present

ROYAL ALBERT ®
ENGLAND
No more Twist
Beatrix Potter
© F. WARNE & CO 1992
© 1992 ROYAL ALBERT LTD

Back Stamp	*Beswick Number*	*Doulton Number*	*U.S. $*	*Price Can. $*	*U.K. £*	*Aust. $*
BP-6	3325	P3325	29.95	49.95	13.50	75.00

OLD MR. BOUNCER™

Modeller: David Lyttleton
Height: 3", 7.6 cm
Colour: Brown jacket and trousers, blue scarf
Issued: 1986 - 1995

BEATRIX POTTER
"Old Mr. Bouncer"
© Frederick Warne & Co. 1986
Licensed by Copyrights
BESWICK ENGLAND

Back Stamp	*Beswick Number*	*Doulton Number*	*U.S. $*	*Price Can. $*	*U.K.£*	*Aust. $*
BP-3	2956	P2956	65.00	90.00	45.00	140.00
BP-4			75.00	110.00	50.00	125.00
BP-6			29.95	49.95	13.50	64.00

OLD MR BROWN™

BEATRIX POTTER'S
"Old Mr Brown"
F. Warne & Co.Ltd.
© Copyright 1963
BESWICK ENGLAND

Modeller:	Albert Hallam
Height:	3 1/4", 8.3 cm
Colour:	Brown owl and red squirrel
Issued:	1963 to the present

Back Stamp	Beswick Number	Doulton Number	U.S. $	Price Can. $	U.K. £	Aust. $
BP-2	1796	P1796	200.00	275.00	95.00	275.00
BP-3			75.00	110.00	45.00	110.00
BP-4			85.00	125.00	50.00	125.00
BP-6			29.95	47.00	13.50	60.00

OLD MR. BROWN CHARACTER JUG™

John Beswick
ENGLAND
BEATRIX POTTER
"Old Mr. Brown"
© 1987 Frederick Warne & Co.
Licensed by Copyrights

Modeller:	Graham Tongue
Height:	3", 7.6 cm
Colour:	Brown and cream
Issued:	1987 - 1992

Back Stamp	Beswick Number	Doulton Number	U.S. $	Price Can. $	U.K.	Aust. $
BP-4	2959	P2959	150.00	200.00	75.00	200.00
BP-6			115.00	150.00	65.00	150.00

OLD MR. PRICKLEPIN™

BEATRIX POTTER'S
"Old Mr Pricklepin"
© Frederick Warne P.L.C. 1983
BESWICK ENGLAND

Modeller:	David Lyttleton
Height:	2 1/2", 6.4 cm
Colour:	Brown hedgehog
Issued:	1983 - 1989

Back Stamp	Beswick Number	Doulton Number	U.S. $	Price Can. $	U.K. £	Aust. $
BP-3	2767	P2767	125.00	170.00	45.00	200.00
BP-4			150.00	200.00	75.00	225.00
BP-6			100.00	130.00	25.00	135.00

PETER AND THE RED POCKET HANDKERCHIEF™

ROYAL ALBERT ®
ENGLAND
Peter and the
Red Pocket Handkerchief
Beatrix Potter
© F. WARNE & CO 1990
© 1990 ROYAL ALBERT LTD

Modeller:	Martyn Alcock
Height:	4 3/4", 12.3 cm
Colour:	Brown blanket, light blue coat
Issued:	1991 to the present

Back Stamp	*Beswick Number*	*Doulton Number*	*U.S. $*	*Price Can. $*	*U.K. £*	*Aust. $*
BP-6	3242	P3242	39.95	59.95	15.95	75.00

PETER ATE A RADISH™

Modeller:	Warren Platt
Height:	4", 10.1 cm
Colour:	Blue jacket, brown and white rabbit, red radishes
Issued:	1995 to the present

Back Stamp	*Beswick Number*	*Doulton Number*	*U.S. $*	*Price Can. $*	*U.K. £*	*Aust. $*
BP-6	3533	P3533	40.00	54.00	16.95	74.00

PETER IN BED™

Modeller:	Martyn C. R. Alcock
Height:	2 3/4", 7.0 cm
Colour:	Blue, white, pink and green
Issued:	1995 to the present

Back Stamp	*Beswick Number*	*Doulton Number*	*U.S. $*	*Price Can. $*	*U.K. £*	*Aust. $*
BP-6	3473	P3473	39.95	65.00	15.95	74.00

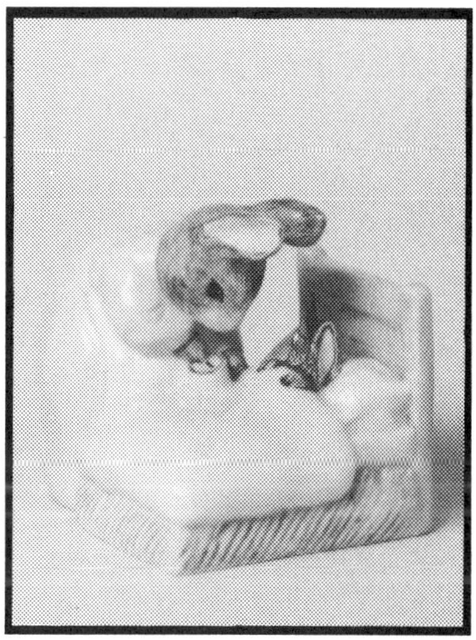

PETER RABBIT™
First Version (Deep Light Blue Jacket)

Modeller:	Arthur Gredington
Height:	4 1/2", 11.4 cm
Colour:	Brown and white rabbit wearing dark blue jacket
Issued:	1948 - c.1980

Back Stamp	*Beswick Number*	*Doulton Number*	*U.S. $*	*Price Can. $*	*U.K. £*	*Aust. $*
BP-1	1091/1	P1091/1	275.00	400.00	145.00	450.00
BP-2			250.00	325.00	125.00	350.00
BP-3			150.00	200.00	75.00	225.00

PETER RABBIT™
Second Version (Pale Light Blue Jacket)

Modeller:	Arthur Gredington
Height:	4 1/2", 11.4 cm
Colour:	Brown and white rabbit wearing light blue jacket
Issued:	c. 1980 to the present

Back Stamp	*Beswick Number*	*Doulton Number*	*U.S. $*	*Price Can. $*	*U.K. £*	*Aust. $*
BP-3	1098/2	P1098/2	65.00	90.00	45.00	100.00
BP-4			75.00	110.00	45.00	125.00
BP-5			100.00	140.00	85.00	150.00
BP-6			29.95	47.00	13.50	57.00

PETER RABBIT™
Third Version (Large size)

Modeller:	Martyn Alcock
Height:	6 3/4", 17.1 cm
Size:	Large
Colour:	Brown rabbit wearing a blue coat
Issued:	1993 to the present

Back Stamp	*Beswick Number*	*Doulton Number*	*U.S. $*	*Price Can. $*	*U.K. £*	*Aust. $*
BP-6	3356	P3356	65.00	91.00	27.00	125.00
BP-7 1993 100th Anniversary			95.00	125.00	50.00	140.00

PETER RABBIT CHARACTER JUG™

John Beswick
ENGLAND
BEATRIX POTTER
"Peter Rabbit"
© 1987 Frederick Warne & Co.
Licensed by Copyrights

Modeller: Graham Tongue
Height: 3", 7.6 cm
Colour: Brown, blue and white
Issued: 1987 - 1992

Back Stamp	*Beswick Number*	*Doulton Number*	*U.S. $*	*Price Can. $*	*U.K. £*	*Aust. $*
BP-4	3006	P3006	150.00	210.00	75.00	225.00
BP-6			115.00	165.00	65.00	175.00

PETER RABBIT IN THE GOOSEBERRY NET™

ROYAL ALBERT ®
ENGLAND
Peter in the Gooseberry Net
Beatrix Potter
© F. WARNE & CO. 1989
© 1989 ROYAL ALBERT LTD

Modeller: David Lyttleton
Height: 2", 4.6 cm
Colour: Brown and white rabbit wearing blue jacket, green netting
Issued: 1989 - 1995

Back Stamp	*Beswick Number*	*Doulton Number*	*U.S. $*	*Price Can. $*	*U.K. £*	*Aust. $*
BP-6	3157	P3157	39.95	69.95	13.95	68.00

PETER RABBIT PLAQUE™
First Version

Modeller: Graham Tongue
Height: 6", 15.2 cm
Colour: Brown rabbit wearing a blue coat
Issued: 1967 - 1969

Photograph not available at press time

Back Stamp	*Beswick Number*	*Doulton Number*	*U.S. $*	*Price Can. $*	*U.K. £*	*Aust. $*
BP-2	2083	P2083		Extremely Rare		400.00

PETER RABBIT PLAQUE™
Second Version

Modeller:	Harry Sales and David Lyttleton
Height:	7 1/2" x 7 1/2", 19.1 cm x 19.1 cm
Colour:	Blue, green, brown and orange
Issued:	1979 - 1983

Back Stamp	*Beswick Number*	*Doulton Number*	*U.S. $*	*Price Can. $*	*U.K. £*	*Aust. $*
BP-3	2650	P2650	145.00	150.00	75.00	150.00

PICKLES™

Modeller:	Albert Hallam
Height:	4 1/2", 11.4 cm
Colour:	Black face dog with brown jacket and white apron, pink book
Issued:	1971 - 1982

Back Stamp	*Beswick Number*	*Doulton Number*	*U.S. $*	*Price Can. $*	*U.K. £*	*Aust. $*
BP-2	2334	P2334	900.00	1,100.00	475.00	800.00
BP-3			475.00	600.00	275.00	650.00

PIGLING BLAND™
First Version (Deep Maroon Jacket)

Modeller:	Graham Orwell
Height:	4 1/4", 10.8 cm
Colour:	Purple jacket, blue waistcoat, yellow trousers
Issued:	1955 - 1974

Back Stamp	*Beswick Number*	*Doulton Number*	*U.S. $*	*Price Can. $*	*U.K. £*	*Aust. $*
BP-2	1365/1	P1365/1	600.00	800.00	275.00	800.00
BP-3			300.00	375.00	200.00	400.00

PIGLING BLAND™
Second Version (Lilac Jacket)

Modeller: Graham Orwell
Height: 4 1/4", 10.8 cm
Colour: Lilac jacket, blue waistcoat, yellow trousers
Issued: c.1972 to the present

Back Stamp	*Beswick Number*	*Doulton Number*	*U.S. $*	*Price Can. $*	*U.K. £*	*Aust. $*
BP-2	1365/2	1365/2	295.00	350.00	175.00	350.00
BP-3			65.00	90.00	50.00	100.00
BP-4			75.00	110.00	60.00	125.00
BP-6			29.95	47.00	13.50	80.00

PIGLING EATS HIS PORRIDGE™

Modeller: Martyn Alcock
Height: 4", 10.1 cm
Colour: Brown coat, blue waistcoat and yellow trousers
Issued: 1991 - 1994

Back Stamp	*Beswick Number*	*Doulton Number*	*U.S. $*	*Price Can. $*	*U.K. £*	*Aust. $*
BP-6	3252	P3252	50.00	70.00	25.00	85.00

PIG-WIG™

Modeller: Albert Hallam
Height: 4", 10.1 cm
Colour: Blue dress with white collar, black pig
Issued: 1972 - 1982

Back Stamp	*Beswick Number*	*Doulton Number*	*U.S. $*	*Price Can. $*	*U.K. £*	*Aust. $*
BP-2	2381	P2382		Extremely Rare		
BP-3			600.00	850.00	400.00	900.00

POORLY PETER RABBIT™

Modeller: David Lyttleton
Height: 3 3/4", 9.5 cm
Colour: Brown-red and white blanket
Issued: 1976 to the present

BEATRIX POTTER
"Poorly Peter Rabbit"
© Frederick Warne & Co. 1976
Licensed by Copyrights
BESWICK ENGLAND

Back Stamp	Beswick Number	Doulton Number	Price U.S. $	Can. $	U.K. £	Aust. $
BP-3	2560	P2560	65.00	90.00	45.00	125.00
BP-4			75.00	110.00	50.00	125.00
BP-6			29.95	47.00	20.00	57.00

REBECCAH PUDDLE-DUCK™

Modeller: David Lyttleton
Height: 3 1/4", 8.3 cm
Colour: White goose, pale blue coat and hat
Issued: 1981 to the present

BEATRIX POTTER'S
Rebeccah Puddle-Duck
F. Warne & Co Ltd.
© Copyright 1981
BESWICK ENGLAND

Back Stamp	Beswick Number	Doulton Number	Price U.S. $	Can. $	U.K. £	Aust.
BP-3	2647	P2647	65.00	90.00	45.00	100.00
BP-4			75.00	110.00	45.00	125.00
BP-6			29.95	47.00	13.50	70.00

RIBBY™

Modeller: Arthur Gredington
Height: 3 1/4", 8.3 cm
Colour: White dress with blue rings, white apron, pink and white striped shawl
Issued: 1951 to the present

BEATRIX POTTER'S
"Ribby"
F. Warne & Co. Ltd.
© Copyright 1951
BESWICK ENGLAND

Back Stamp	Beswick Number	Doulton Number	Price U.S. $	Can. $	U.K. £	Aust. $
BP-1	1199	P1199	300.00	400.00	200.00	450.00
BP-2			225.00	300.00	125.00	325.00
BP-3			65.00	90.00	45.00	100.00
BP-4			75.00	110.00	55.00	125.00
BP-6			29.95	47.00	13.50	57.00

Note: Name shown as "Mrs Ribby" on BP-6.

ROYAL ALBERT
ENGLAND
Ribby and
the patty pan
Beatrix Potter
© F WARNE & CO 1991
© 1992 ROYAL ALBERT LTD

RIBBY AND THE PATTY PAN™

Modeller: Martyn Alcock
Height: 3 1/2", 8.9 cm
Colour: Blue dress, white apron
Issued: 1992 to the present

Back Stamp	*Beswick Number*	*Doulton Number*	*U.S. $*	*Price Can. $*	*U.K. £*	*Aust. $*
BP-6	3280	P3280	29.95	49.95	13.50	65.00

SALLY HENNY PENNY™

Modeller: Albert Hallam
Height: 4", 10.1 cm
Colour: Brown and gold chicken, black hat and cloak, two yellow chicks
Issued: 1974 - 1993

BEATRIX POTTER'S
Sally Henny Penny
F. Warne & Co.Ltd.
© Copyright 1974
BESWICK ENGLAND

Back Stamp	*Beswick Number*	*Doulton Number*	*U.S. $*	*Price Can. $*	*U.K. £*	*Aust. $*
BP-3	2452	P2452	65.00	90.00	50.00	100.00
BP-4			75.00	110.00	50.00	125.00
BP-6			45.00	60.00	20.00	84.00

Note: The confirmation of the two versions of Sally Henny Penny is still lacking. We are not able to distinguish the differences between a first and second version let alone photograph them. We have removed the versions at this time until a true definition can be shown.

BEATRIX POTTERS

SAMUEL WHISKERS™

Modeller: Arthur Gredington
Height: 3 1/4", 8.3 cm
Colour: Light green coat, yellow waistcoat and trousers
Issued: 1948 - 1995

Back Stamp	*Beswick Number*	*Doulton Number*	*U.S. $*	*Price Can. $*	*U.K. £*	*Aust. $*
BP-1	1106	P1106	300.00	425.00	130.00	450.00
BP-2			275.00	350.00	115.00	375.00
BP-3			65.00	90.00	45.00	100.00
BP-4			75.00	110.00	45.00	125.00
BP-6			29.95	49.95	13.50	57.00

SIMPKIN™

Modeller: Alan Maslankowski
Height: 4", 10.1 cm
Colour: Green coat
Issued: 1975 - 1983

BEATRIX POTTER'S
"Simpkin"
F. Warne & Co.Ltd.
© Copyright 1975
BESWICK ENGLAND

Back Stamp	Beswick Number	Doulton Number	Price U.S. $	Can. $	U.K. £	Aust. $
BP-3	2508	P2508	900.00	1,200.00	525.00	900.00

SIR ISAAC NEWTON™

Modeller: Graham Tongue
Height: 3 3/4", 9.5 cm
Colour: Pale green jacket yellow waistcoat with tan markings
Issued: 1973 - 1984

BEATRIX POTTER'S
"Sir Isaac Newton"
F. Warne & Co. Ltd.
© Copyright 1973
BESWICK
MADE IN ENGLAND

Back Stamp	Beswick Number	Doulton Number	Price U.S. $	Can. $	U.K. £	Aust. $
BP-3	2425	P2425	600.00	675.00	300.00	650.00

SQUIRREL NUTKIN™
First Version (Red Brown Squirrel)

Modeller: Arthur Gredington
Height: 3 3/4", 9.5 cm
Colour: Red-brown squirrel holding green-brown nut
Issued: 1948 - c.1980

BEATRIX POTTER'S
BESWICK ENGLAND

Back Stamp	Beswick Number	Doulton Number	Price U.S. $	Can. $	U.K. £	Aust. $
BP-1	1102	P1102/1	275.00	350.00	150.00	400.00
BP-2			250.00	300.00	125.00	325.00
BP-3			150.00	200.00	95.00	225.00

SQUIRREL NUTKIN™
Second Version (Golden Brown Squirrel)

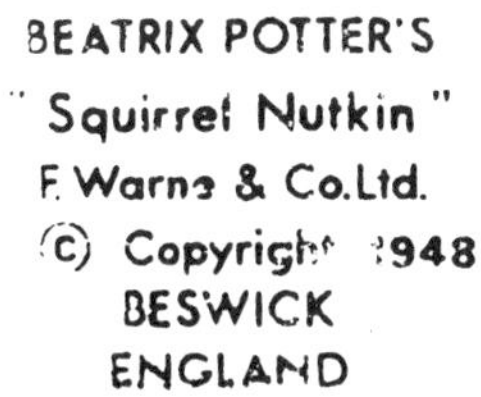

Modeller:	Arthur Gredington
Height:	3 3/4", 9.5 cm
Colour:	Golden-brown squirrel holding green nut
Issued:	c.1980 to the present

Back Stamp	*Beswick Number*	*Doulton Number*	*U.S. $*	*Price Can. $*	*U.K. £*	*Aust. $*
BP-3	1102	P1102/2	65.00	90.00	40.00	100.00
BP-4			75.00	110.00	45.00	125.00
BP-6			29.95	47.00	13.50	64.00

SUSAN™

Modeller:	David Lyttleton
Height:	4", 10.1 cm
Colour:	Blue dress, green, pink and black shawl and hat
Issued:	1983 - 1989

Back Stamp	*Beswick Number*	*Doulton Number*	*U.S. $*	*Price Can. $*	*U.K. £*	*Aust. $*
BP-3	2716	P2716	225.00	275.00	110.00	300.00
BP-4			200.00	225.00	85.00	125.00
BP-6			150.00	200.00	75.00	200.00

TABITHA TWITCHIT™
First Version (Blue Striped Top)

Modeller:	Arthur Gredington
Height:	3 1/2", 8.9 cm
Colour:	Blue and white striped dress, white apron
Issued:	1961 - 1974

Back Stamp	*Beswick Number*	*Doulton Number*	*U.S. $*	*Price Can. $*	*U.K. £*	*Aust. $*
BP-2	1676/1	P1676/1	375.00	425.00	150.00	400.00
BP-3			275.00	350.00	125.00	375.00

TABITHA TWITCHETT™
Second Version (White Top)

Modeller: Arthur Gredington
Height: 3 1/2", 8.9 cm
Colour: Blue and white striped dress, white apron
Issued: c.1970 - 1995

BEATRIX POTTER'S
"Tabitha Twitchett"
F. Warne & Co.Ltd.
© Copyright 1961
BESWICK ENGLAND

Note: BP-3 and forward has Twitchett spelt with two "T"s

Back Stamp	*Beswick Number*	*Doulton Number*	*U.S. $*	*Price Can. $*	*U.K. £*	*Aust. $*
BP-2	1676/2	P1676/2	250.00	325.00	140.00	300.00
BP-3			65.00	90.00	45.00	100.00
BP-4			75.00	110.00	50.00	125.00
BP-6			29.95	47.00	13.50	64.00

TABITHA TWITCHIT AND MISS MOPPET™

Modeller: David Lyttleton
Height: 3 1/2", 8.9 cm
Colour: Lilac dress, white apron, yellow sponge and puffee
Issued: 1976 - 1993

BEATRIX POTTER'S
Tabitha Twitchit and Miss Moppet
F. Warne & Co.Ltd.
© Copyright 1976
BESWICK ENGLAND

Back Stamp	*Beswick Number*	*Doulton Number*	*U.S. $*	*Price Can. $*	*U.K. £*	*Aust. $*
BP-3	2544	P2544	200.00	275.00	100.00	300.00
BP-4			250.00	350.00	90.00	375.00
BP-6			75.00	110.00	35.00	125.00

TAILOR OF GLOUCESTER™
First Version (Small size)

Modeller: Arthur Gredington
Height: 3 1/2", 8.9 cm
Colour: Brown mouse, yellow bobbin of red thread
Issued: 1949 to the present

BEATRIX POTTERS
Tailor of Gloucester
BESWICK ENGLAND
F. WARNE & CO. LTD.
COPYRIGHT

Back Stamp	*Beswick Number*	*Doulton Number*	*U.S. $*	*Price Can. $*	*U.K. £*	*Aust. $*
BP-1	1108/1	P1108/1	300.00	450.00	200.00	475.00
BP-2			250.00	350.00	100.00	375.00
BP-3			65.00	90.00	45.00	100.00
BP-4			75.00	110.00	45.00	125.00
BP-6			29.95	49.95	13.50	57.00

TAILOR OF GLOUCESTER™
Second Version (Large size)

Modeller: Arthur Gredington
Height: 6", 15.0 cm
Colour: Brown mouse, yellow bobbin of red thread
Issued: 1995 to the present

Back Stamp	*Beswick Number*	*Doulton Number*	*U.S. $*	*Price Can. $*	*U.K. £*	*Aust. $*
BP-6	3449	P3449	65.00	91.00	27.00	125.00

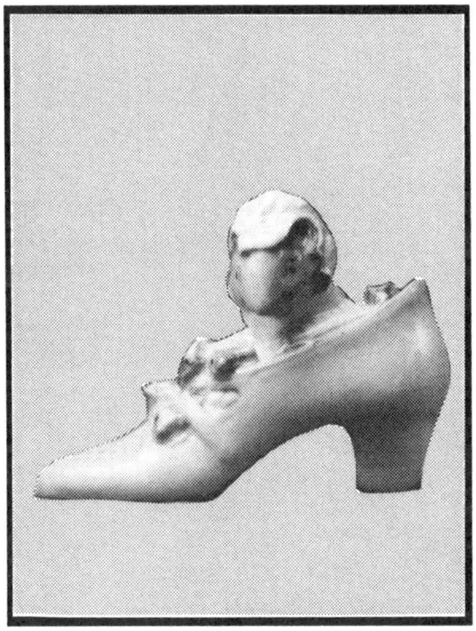

THE OLD WOMAN WHO LIVED IN A SHOE™

Modeller: Colin Melbourne
Height: 2 3/4" x 3 3/4", 7 cm x 9.5 cm
Colour: Blue shoe
Issued: 1959 to the present

Back Stamp	*Beswick Number*	*Doulton Number*	*U.S. $*	*Price Can. $*	*U.K. £*	*Aust. $*
BP-2	1545	P1545	225.00	300.00	95.00	325.00
BP-3			65.00	90.00	45.00	90.00
BP-4			75.00	110.00	50.00	110.00
BP-6			29.95	49.95	13.50	84.00

THE OLD WOMAN WHO LIVED IN A SHOE KNITTING™

Modeller: David Lyttleton
Height: 3", 7.5 cm
Colour: Purple dress, white apron, pale blue shawl and mob cap, yellow chair
Issued: 1983 to the present

BEATRIX POTTER
"The Old Woman who lived
in a Shoe.
"Knitting"
© Frederick Warne & Co. 1983
Licensed by Copyrights
BESWICK ENGLAND

Back Stamp	*Beswick Number*	*Doulton Number*	*U.S. $*	*Price Can. $*	*U.K.£*	*Aust. $*
BP-3	2804	P2804	250.00	350.00	145.00	345.00
BP-4			275.00	375.00	145.00	400.00
BP-6			29.95	47.00	13.50	64.00

THOMASINA TITTLEMOUSE™

Modeller: David Lyttleton
Height: 3 1/4", 8.3 cm
Colour: Brown and pink Highlights
Issued: 1981 - 1989

Correct	Error
BEATRIX POTTER'S "Thomasina Tittlemouse" F. Warne & Co Ltd. © Copyright 1981 BESWICK ENGLAND	BEATRIX POTTER "Tomasina Tittlemouse" © Frederick Warne & Co. 1981 Licensed by Copyrights BESWICK ENGLAND

Backstamp Variations

Back Stamp	Beswick Number	Doulton Number	U.S. $	Price Can. $	U.K. £	Aust. $
BP-3 Error	2668	P2668	125.00	175.00	50.00	240.00
BP-3 Corrected			125.00	175.00	50.00	240.00
BP-4			150.00	200.00	50.00	225.00
BP-6			100.00	65.00	35.00	64.00

TIMMY TIPTOES™

First Version (Red Jacket - Brown-grey Squirrel)

Modeller: Arthur Gredington
Height: 3 3/4", 9.5 cm
Colour: Var. 1 —Brown grey squirrel; red jacket
Var. 2 — Grey squirrel; red jaacket
Issued: 1948 - c.1980

BEATRIX POTTER'S
Timmy Tiptoes
F. WARNE & CO. LTD. COPYRIGHT
BESWICK ENGLAND

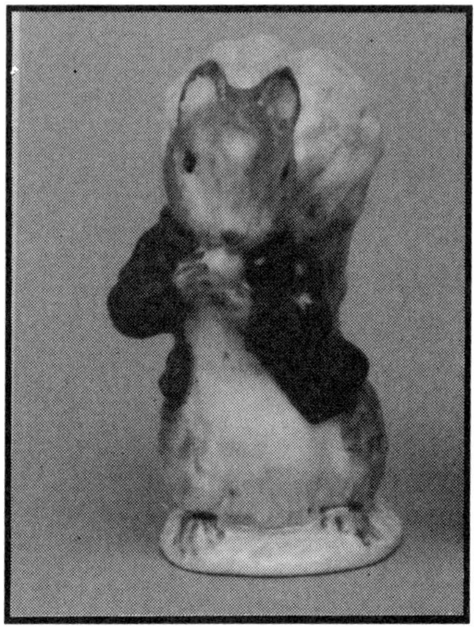

Back Stamp	Beswick Number	Doulton Number	U.S. $	Price Can. $	U.K. £	Aust. $
BP-1	1101/1	P1101/1	250.00	350.00	125.00	375.00
BP-2			225.00	300.00	115.00	325.00
BP-3	Brown-grey squirrel		150.00	200.00	85.00	225.00
BP-3	Grey squirrel		150.00	200.00	85.00	225.00

TIMMY TIPTOES™

Third Version (Light Pink Jacket - Grey Squirrel)

Modeller: Arthur Gredington
Height: 3 1/2", 8.9 cm
Colour: Grey squirrel wearing pink jacket
Issued: c.1980 to the present

BEATRIX POTTER'S
"Timmy Tiptoes"
F. Warne & Co.Ltd.
(c) Copyright 1948
BESWICK ENGLAND

Back Stamp	Beswick Number	Doulton Number	U.S. $	Price Can. $	U.K. £	Aust. $
BP-3	1101/2	P1101/2	65.00	90.00	40.00	125.00
BP-4			75.00	110.00	45.00	125.00
BP-6			29.95	47.00	13.50	64.00

TIMMY WILLIE FROM JOHNNY TOWN-MOUSE™

Modeller: Arthur Gredington
Height: 2 1/2", 6.4 cm
Colour: Brown and white mouse, green base
Issued: 1949 - 1993

Back Stamp	*Beswick Number*	*Doulton Number*	*U.S. $*	*Price Can. $*	*U.K. £*	*Aust. $*
BP-1	1109	P1109	250.00	350.00	125.00	375.00
BP-2			225.00	300.00	115.00	325.00
BP-3			65.00	90.00	50.00	100.00
BP-4			75.00	110.00	55.00	125.00
BP-6			45.00	49.95	25.00	57.00

TIMMY WILLIE SLEEPING™

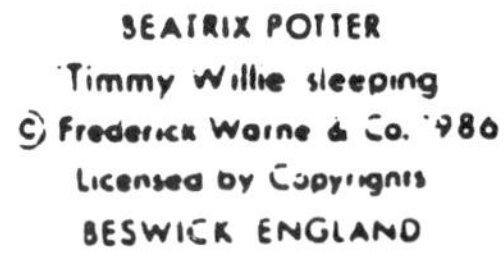

Modeller: Graham Tongue
Height: 1 1/4" x 3 3/4", 3.2 cm x 9.5 cm
Colour: Green, white and brown
Issued: 1986 to the present

Back Stamp	*Beswick Number*	*Doulton Number*	*U.S. $*	*Price Can. $*	*U.K. £*	*Aust. $*
BP-3	2996	P2996	175.00	250.00	115.00	275.00
BP-4			200.00	275.00	125.00	300.00
BP-6			29.95	47.00	13.50	64.00

TOM KITTTEN™
First Version (Deep Light Blue Outfit)

Modeller: Arthur Gredington
Height: 3 1/2", 8.9 cm
Colour: Tabby kitten wearing deep light blue trousers and jacket; dark green base
Issued: 1948-c.1980

Back Stamp	*Beswick Number*	*Doulton Number*	*U.S. $*	*Price Can. $*	*U.K. £*	*Aus.t $*
BP-1	1100	P1100/1	275.00	400.00	125.00	425.00
BP-2			225.00	300.00	115.00	325.00
BP-3			65.00	90.00	45.00	120.00

TOM KITTEN™
Second Version (Pale Light Blue Outfit)

Modeller: Arthur Gredington
Height: 3 1/2", 8.9 cm
Colour: Tabby kitten wearing pale light blue trousers and jacket; light green base
Issued: c.1980 to the present

Back Stamp	*Beswick Number*	*Doulton Number*	*U.S. $*	*Price Can. $*	*U.K. £*	*Aust. $*
BP-3	1100	P1100/2	65.00	90.00	45.00	100.00
BP-4			75.00	110.00	55.00	125.00
BP-6			29.95	47.00	13.50	57.00

TOM KITTEN™
Third Version (Large size)

Modeller: Martyn Alcock
Height: 5 1/4", 13.3 cm
Colour: Tabby kitten wearing light blue trousers and jacket; light green base
Issued: 1994 to the present

Back Stamp	*Beswick Number*	*Doulton Number*	*U.S. $*	*Price Can. $*	*U.K. £*	*Aus.t $*
BP-	3405	P3405	65.00	91.00	25.95	125.00

TOM KITTEN AND BUTTERFLY™

Modeller: Ted Chawner
Height: 3 1/2", 8.9 cm
Colour: Blue outfit, yellow hat
Issued: 1987 - 1994

Back Stamp	*Beswick Number*	*Doulton Number*	*U.S. $*	*Price Can. $*	*U.K. £*	*Aust. $*
BP-3	3030	P3030	225.00	300.00	175.00	325.00
BP-4			250.00	350.00	175.00	375.00
BP-6			100.00	115.00	20.00	90.00

TOM KITTEN CHARACTER JUG™

Modeller: Ted Chawner
Height: 3", 7.6 cm
Colour: Brown, blue and white
Issued: 1989 - 1992

Back Stamp	Beswick Number	Doulton Number	U.S. $	Price Can. $	U.K. £	Aust. $
BP-4	3103	P3103	150.00	200.00	75.00	100.00
BP-6			115.00	150.00	65.00	80.00

Photograph not available at press time

TOM KITTEN PLAQUE™

Modeller: Graham Tongue
Height: 6", 15.2 cm
Colour: Unknown
Issued: 1967 - 1969

Back Stamp	Beswick Number	Doulton Number	U.S. $	Price Can. $	U.K.	Aust. $
BP-2	2085	P2085		Extremely Rare		

TOM THUMB™

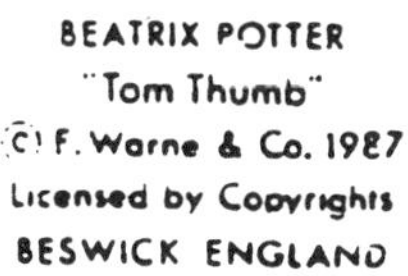

Modeller: Warren Platt
Height: 3 1/4", 8.3 cm
Colour: Rose-pink and yellow chimney
Issued: 1987 to the present

Back Stamp	Beswick Number	Doulton Number	U.S. $	Price Can. $	U.K. £	Aust. $
BP-3	2989	P2989	165.00	225.00	85.00	225.00
BP-4			165.00	225.00	85.00	250.00
BP-6			29.95	47.00	13.50	64.00

TOMMY BROCK™
First Version (Handle Out, Small Eye Patch)™

Modeller: Graham Orwell
Height: 3 1/2", 8.9 cm
Colour: Blue jacket, pink waistcoat, yellow-green trousers
Issued: 1955 - 1974

BEATRIX POTTER'S
"Tommy Brock"
F. Warne & Co Ltd.
© Copyright 1955
BESWICK ENGLAND

Back Stamp	Beswick Number	Doulton Number	U.S. $	Price Can. $	U.K. £	Aust. $
BP-2	1348/1	P1348/1	625.00	900.00	275.00	700.00
BP-3			525.00	800.00	250.00	900.00

TOMMY BROCK™
Second Version (Handle Out, Large Eye Patch)

Modeller: Graham Orwell
Height: 3 1/2", 8.9 cm
Colour: Blue jacket, pink waistcoat, yellow trousers
Issued: c.1970 - c.1980

BEATRIX POTTER'S
"Tommy Brock"
F. Warne & Co.Ltd.
© Copyright 1955
BESWICK ENGLAND

Back Stamp	Beswick Number	Doulton Number	U.S. $	Price Can. $	U.K. £	Aust. $
BP-2	1348/2	P1348/2	625.00	900.00	275.00	700.00
BP-3			525.00	800.00	250.00	900.00

TOMMY BROCK™
Third Version (Handle in, Small Eye Patch)

Modeller: Graham Orwell
Height: 3 1/2", 8.9 cm
Colour: Blue-grey jacket, pink waistcoat, yellow trousers
Issued: c.1980 - Unknown

BEATRIX POTTER'S
"Tommy Brock"
F. Warne & Co.Ltd.
© Copyright 1955
BESWICK ENGLAND

Back Stamp	Beswick Number	Doulton Number	U.S. $	Price Can. $	U.K. £	Aust. $
BP-3			65.00	90.00	45.00	100.00

TOMMY BROCK™
Fourth Version (Handle in, Large Eye Patch)

Modeller: Graham Orwell
Height: 3 1/2", 8.9 cm
Colour: Blue-grey jacket, red waistcoat, yellow trousers
Issued: c.1980 to the present

Back Stamp	*Beswick Number*	*Doulton Number*	*U.S. $*	*Price Can. $*	*U.K. £*	*Aust. $*
BP-3	1348	P1348/4	65.00	90.00	45.00	125.00
BP-4			75.00	110.00	50.00	125.00
BP-6			29.95	49.95	13.50	68.00

TREE LAMP BASE™

Modeller: James Hayward and Albert Hallam
Height: 7", 17.8 cm
Colour: Brown and green
Issued: 1958 - 1982

Back Stamp	*Beswick Number*	*Doulton Number*	*U.S. $*	*Price Can. $*	*U.K. £*	*Aust. $*
BP-2	1531	P1531	275.00	375.00	175.00	400.00
BP-3			225.00	300.00	125.00	325.00

BEATRIX POTTER
STUDIO SCULPTURES

Photograph not available at press time

SS1
TIMMY WILLIE™

Designer: Harry Sales
Modeller: Graham Tongue
Height: 4 1/4", 10.8 cm
Colour: Green and brown
Issued: 1985 - 1985

Beswick Number	*U.S. $*	*Price Can. $*	*U.K. £*	*Aust. $*
SS1	90.00	100.00	65.00	120.00

SS2
FLOPSY BUNNIES™

Designer: Harry Sales
Modeller: Graham Tongue
Height: 5", 12.7 cm
Colour: Browns and green
Issued: 1985 - 1985

Beswick Number	*U.S. $*	*Price Can. $*	*U.K. £*	*Aust. $*
SS2	90.00	100.00	65.00	120.00

SS3
MR. JEREMY FISHER™

Designer: Harry Sales
Modeller: David Lyttleton
Height: 4", 10.1 cm
Colour: Beige, cream and cream
Issued: 1985 - 1985

Beswick Number	*U.S. $*	*Price Can. $*	*U.K. £*	*Aust. $*
SS3	100.00	125.00	75.00	135.00

SS4
PETER RABBIT™

Designer: Harry Sales
Modeller: Graham Tongue
Height: 7", 17.8 cm
Colour: Browns, blue and green
Issued: 1985 - 1985

Beswick Number	*U.S. $*	*Price Can. $*	*U.K. £*	*Aust. $*
SS4	100.00	125.00	75.00	135.00

SS11
MRS. TIGGY WINKLE™

Designer: Harry Sales
Modeller: Graham Tongue
Height: 5", 12.7 cm
Colour: Browns, green, white and blue
Issued: 1985 - 1985

Beswick Number	*U.S. $*	*Price Can. $*	*U.K. £*	*Aust. $*
SS11	100.00	125.00	75.00	135.00

SS26
YOCK YOCK™
(In The Tub)

Designer: Harry Sales
Modeller: David Lyttleton
Height: 1 7/8", 5.0 cm
Colour: Pink and brown
Issued: 1986 - 1986

Beswick Number	*U.S. $*	*Price Can. $*	*U.K. £*	*Aust. $*
SS26	240.00	275.00	150.00	295.00

Photograph not available at press time

Photograph not available at press time

SS27
PETER RABBIT™
(In The Watering Can)

Designer:	Harry Sales
Modeller:	David Lyttleton
Height:	3 1/4", 8.3 cm
Colour:	Browns and blue
Issued:	1986 - 1986

Beswick Number	*U.S. $*	*Price Can. $*	*U.K. £*	*Aust. $*
SS27	270.00	300.00	175.00	325.00

BEDTIME CHORUS

1801
PIANIST™

Designer: Albert Hallam
Height: 3", 7.6 cm
Colour: Pale blue and yellow
Issued: 1962-1969

Beswick Number	*U.S. $*	*Price Can. $*	*U.K. £*	*Aust. $*
1801	140.00	175.00	80.00	130.00

1802
PIANO™

Designer: Albert Hallam
Height: 3", 7.6 cm
Colour: Brown and white
Issued: 1962-1969

Beswick Number	*U.S. $*	*Price Can. $*	*U.K. £*	*Aust. $*
1802	125.00	150.00	50.00	130.00

1803
CAT - SINGING™

Designer: Albert Hallam
Height: 1 1/4", 3.2 cm
Colour: Ginger stripe
Issued: 1962-1971

Beswick Number	*U.S. $*	*Price Can. $*	*U.K. £*	*Aust. $*
1803	75.00	100.00	50.00	130.00

1804
BOY WITHOUT SPECTACLES™

Designer: Albert Hallam
Height: 3 1/2", 8.9 cm
Colour: Yellow, white and blue
Issued: 1962-1969

Beswick Number	*U.S. $*	*Price Can. $*	*U.K. £*	*Aust. $*
1804	250.00	275.00	115.00	130.00

1805
BOY WITH SPECTACLES™

Designer: Albert Hallam
Height: 3", 7.6 cm
Colour: Green, white and blue
Issued: 1962-1969

Beswick Number	*U.S. $*	*Price Can. $*	*U.K. £*	*Aust. $*
1805	300.00	350.00	160.00	130.00

1824
DOG - SINGING™

Designer: Albert Hallam
Height: 1 1/2", 3.8 cm
Colour: Tan
Issued: 1962-1971

Beswick Number	*U.S. $*	*Price Can. $*	*U.K. £*	*Aust. $*
1824	70.00	90.00	45.00	140.00

1825
BOY WITH GUITAR™

Designer: Albert Hallam
Height: 3", 7.6 cm
Colour: Blue-grey, brown and blue
Issued: 1962-1969

Beswick Number	*U.S. $*	*Price Can. $*	*U.K. £*	*Aust. $*
1825	250.00	275.00	115.00	140.00

1826
GIRL WITH HARP™

Designer: Albert Hallam
Height: 3 1/2", 8.9 cm
Colour: Purple, red and brown
Issued: 1962-1969

Beswick Number	*U.S. $*	*Price Can. $*	*U.K. £*	*Aust. $*
1826	250.00	275.00	115.00	140.00

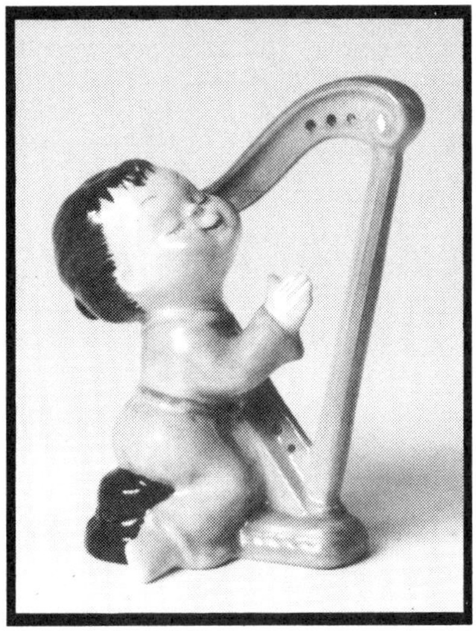

BESWICK BEARS

BB001
WILLIAM™

Designer:	Unknown
Height:	2 1/4", 5.7 cm
Colour:	Brown bear; blue apron; white and rose book
Issued:	1993-1993

Beswick Number	*U.S. $*	*Price Can. $*	*U.K. £*	*Aust. $*
BB001	25.00	35.00	15.00	35.00

BB002
BILLY™

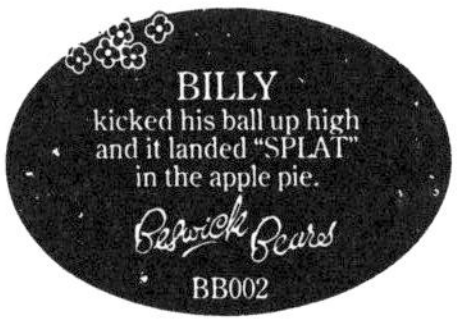

Designer:	Unknown
Height:	4", 10.1 cm
Colour:	Brown bear; green waistcoat; blue hat; yellow, red and blue ball
Issued:	1993-1993

Beswick Number	*U.S. $*	*Price Can. $*	*U.K. £*	*Aust. $*
BB002	25.00	35.00	15.00	35.00

BB003
HARRY™

Designer:	Unknown
Height:	3 1/4", 8.3 cm
Colour:	Brown bear; blue waistcoat; brown hat; white plates
Issued:	1993-1993

Beswick Number	*U.S. $*	*Price Can. $*	*U.K. £*	*Aust. $*
BB003	25.00	35.00	15.00	35.00

BB004
BOBBY™

Designer: Unknown
Height: 4", 10.1 cm
Colour: Brown bear; blue waistcoat; brown hat; yellow ball; black and red bat
Issued: 1993-1993

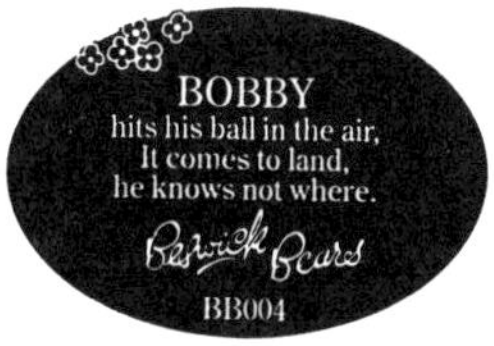

Beswick Number	*U.S. $*	*Can. $*	*U.K. £*	*Aust. $*
BB004	25.00	35.00	15.00	35.00

BB005
JAMES™

Designer: Unknown
Height: 3 3/4", 9.5 cm
Colour: Brown bear; yellow waistcoat; blue hat; blue parcel with pink ribbon
Issued: 1993-1993

Beswick Number	*U.S. $*	*Can. $*	*U.K. £*	*Aust. $*
BB005	25.00	35.00	15.00	35.00

BB006
SUSIE™

Designer: Unknown
Height: 3 1/2", 8.9 cm
Colour: Brown bear; blue dress; brown recorder
Issued: 1993-1993

Beswick Number	*U.S. $*	*Can. $*	*U.K. £*	*Aust. $*
BB006	25.00	35.00	15.00	35.00

BB007
ANGELA™

Designer:	Unknown
Height:	3 1/4", 8.3 cm
Colour:	Brown bear; yellow dress; white flowers
Issued:	1993-1993

Beswick Number	*U.S. $*	*Price Can. $*	*U.K. £*	*Aust. $*
BB007	25.00	35.00	15.00	35.00

BB008
CHARLOTTE™

Designer:	Unknown
Height:	4", 10.1 cm
Colour:	Brown bear; pink dress; blue and yellow parasol
Issued:	1993-1993

Beswick Number	*U.S. $*	*Price Can. $*	*U.K. £*	*Aust. $*
BB008	25.00	35.00	15.00	35.00

BB009
SAM™

Designer:	Unknown
Height:	3 1/2", 8.9
Colour:	Brown bear; rose waistcoat; yellow banjo
Issued:	1993-1993

Beswick Number	*U.S. $*	*Price Can. $*	*U.K. £*	*Aust. $*
BB009	25.00	35.00	15.00	35.00

BB010
LIZZY™

Designer:	Unknown
Height:	2 1/4", 5.7 cm
Colour:	Brown bear; pink dress; paint box
Issued:	1993-1993

Beswick Number	*U.S. $*	*Price Can. $*	*U.K. £*	*Aust. $*
BB010	25.00	35.00	15.00	35.00

BB011
EMILY™

Designer:	Unknown
Height:	3 1/2", 8.9 cm
Colour:	Brown bear; pale blue dress; brown picnic hamper
Issued:	1993-1993

Beswick Number	*U.S. $*	*Price Can. $*	*U.K. £*	*Aust. $*
BB011	25.00	35.00	15.00	35.00

BB012
SARAH™

Designer:	Unknown
Height:	3 1/4", 8.3 cm
Colour:	Brown bear; green dress; white cup and saucer
Issued:	1993-1993

Beswick Number	*U.S. $*	*Price Can. $*	*U.K. £*	*Aust. $*
BB012	25.00	35.00	15.00	35.00

BRAMBLY HEDGE

DBH1
POPPY EYEBRIGHT™

Designer:	Harry Sales
Modeller:	David Lyttleton
Height:	3 1/4", 9.5 cm
Colour:	Grey-white and pink dress, white apron trimmed with blue flowers
Issued:	1982 to the present

Back Stamp	*U.S. $*	*Price Can. $*	*U.K. £*	*Aust. $*
BH-1	40.00	55.00	15.95	64.00

DBH2
MR. APPLE™

Designer:	Harry Sales
Modeller:	David Lyttleton
Height:	3 1/4", 8.3 cm
Colour:	Black trousers, white and blue striped shirt, white apron
Issued:	1982 to the present

Back Stamp	*U.S. $*	*Price Can. $*	*U.K. £*	*Aust. $*
BH-1	40.00	55.00	14.95	64.00

DBH3
MRS. APPLE™

Designer:	Harry Sales
Modeller:	David Lyttleton
Height:	3 1/4", 8.3 cm
Colour:	White and blue striped dress, white apron
Issued:	1982 to the present

Back Stamp	*U.S. $*	*Price Can. $*	*U.K. £*	*Aust. $*
BH-1	40.00	55.00	14.95	64.00

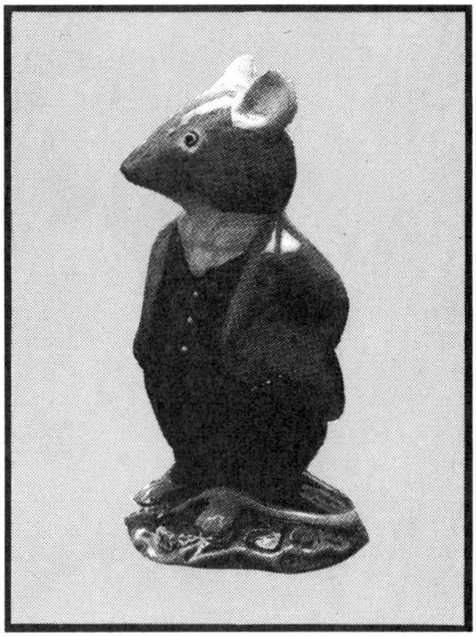

DBH4
LORD WOODMOUSE™

Designer: Harry Sales
Modeller: David Lyttleton
Height: 3 1/4", 8.3 cm
Colour: Green trousers, brown coat and burgundy waistcoat
Issued: 1982 to the present

Back Stamp	U.S. $	Price Can. $	U.K. £	Aust. $
BH-1	40.00	55.00	15.95	64.00

DBH5
LADY WOODMOUSE™

Designer: Harry Sales
Modeller: David Lyttleton
Height: 3 1/4", 8.3 cm
Colour: Red and white striped dress, white apron
Issued: 1982 to the present

Back Stamp	U.S. $	Price Can. $	U.K. £	Aust. $
BH-1	25.00	55.00	15.95	64.00

DBH6
DUSTY DOGWOOD™

Designer: Harry Sales
Modeller: David Lyttleton
Height: 3 1/4", 8.3 cm
Colour: Dark grey suit, red waistcoat
Issued: 1982 to the present

Back Stamp	U.S. $	Price Can. $	U.K. £	Aust. $
BH-1	40.00	55.00	14.95	64.00

DBH7
WILFRED TOADFLAX™

Designer:	Harry Sales
Modeller:	David Lyttleton
Height:	3 1/4", 8.3 cm
Colour:	Grey trousers, red and white striped shirt
Issued:	1982 to the present

Back Stamp	*U.S. $*	*Price Can. $*	*U.K. £*	*Aust. $*
BH-1	38.00	55.00	14.95	64.00

DBH8
PRIMROSE WOODMOUSE™

Designer:	Harry Sales
Modeller:	David Lyttleton
Height:	3 1/4", 8.3 cm
Colour:	Yellow dress with white apron
Issued:	1982 to the present

Back Stamp	*U.S. $*	*Price Can. $*	*U.K. £*	*Aust. $*
BH-1	38.00	55.00	14.95	64.00

DBH9
OLD MRS. EYEBRIGHT™

Designer:	Harry Sales
Modeller:	David Lyttleton
Height:	3 1/4, 8.3 cm"
Colour:	Mauve skirt, white and pink striped shawl, white apron
Issued:	1983 to the present

Back Stamp	*U.S. $*	*Price Can. $*	*U.K. £*	*Aust. $*
BH-1	40.00	55.00	15.95	64.00

DBH10
MR. TOADFLAX™

Designer: Harry Sales
Modeller: David Lyttleton
Height: 3 1/4", 8.3 cm
Colour: Blue and white striped shirt, pink trousers
Issued: 1983 to the present

Back Stamp	*U.S. $*	*Price Can. $*	*U.K. £*	*Aust. $*
BH-1	40.00	55.00	15.95	64.00

DBH11
MRS. TOADFLAX™

Designer: Harry Sales
Modeller: David Lyttleton
Height: 3 1/4", 8.3 cm
Colour: Green and white striped dress, white apron
Issued: 1985 to the present

Back Stamp	*U.S. $*	*Price Can. $*	*U.K. £*	*Aust. $*
BH-1	40.00	55.00	15.95	64.00

DBH12
CATKIN™

Designer: Harry Sales
Modeller: David Lyttleton
Height: 3 1/4", 8.3 cm
Colour: Yellow dress with white apron
Issued: 1985 - 1994

Back Stamp	*U.S. $*	*Price Can. $*	*U.K. £*	*Aust. $*
BH-1	34.00	55.00	14.95	64.00

DBH13
OLD VOLE™

Designer:	Harry Sales
Modeller:	David Lyttleton
Height:	3 1/4", 8.3 cm
Colour:	Green jacket,blue trousers, yellow waistcoat
Issued:	1985 - 1992

Royal Doulton®
OLD VOLE
D.B.H. 13
FROM THE BRAMBLY HEDGE
GIFT COLLECTION
© 1986 JILL BARKLEM

Back Stamp	*U.S. $*	*Price Can. $*	*U.K. £*	*Aust. $*
BH-1	75.00	100.00	40.00	75.00

DBH14
BASIL™

Designer:	Harry Sales
Modeller:	David Lyttleton
Height:	3 1/4", 8.3 cm
Colour:	Brown waistcoat, green and white striped trousers
Issued:	1985 - 1992

Royal Doulton®
BASIL
D.B.H. 14
FROM THE BRAMBLY HEDGE
GIFT COLLECTION
© 1986 JILL BARKLEM

Back Stamp	*U.S. $*	*Price Can. $*	*U.K. £*	*Aust. $*
BH-1	75.00	100.00	40.00	75.00

DBH15
MRS. CRUSTYBREAD™

Designer:	Graham Tongue
Modeller:	Ted Chawner
Height:	3 1/4", 8.3 cm
Colour:	Yellow dress, white apron and cap
Issued:	1987 - 1994

Royal Doulton®
MRS. CRUSTYBREAD
D.B.H. 15
FROM THE BRAMBLY HEDGE
GIFT COLLECTION
© 1987 JILL BARKLEM

Back Stamp	*U.S. $*	*Price Can. $*	*U.K. £*	*Aust. $*
BH-1	34.00	52.00	25.00	64.00

DBH16
CLOVER™

Designer: Graham Tongue
Modeller: Graham Tongue
Height: 3 1/4", 8.3 cm
Colour: Burgundy dress, white apron
Issued: 1987 to the present

Royal Doulton®
CLOVER
DBH 16
FROM THE BRAMBLY HEDGE
GIFT COLLECTION
© 1987 JILL BARKLEM

Back Stamp	*U.S. $*	*Can. $*	*U.K. £*	*Aust. $*
BH-1	34.00	55.00	14.95	64.00

DBH17
TEASEL™

Designer: Graham Tongue
Modeller: Ted Chawner
Height: 3 1/4", 8.3 cm
Colour: Blue-grey dungarees, blue and white striped shirt
Issued: 1987 - 1993

Royal Doulton®
TEASEL
DBH 17
FROM THE BRAMBLY HEDGE
GIFT COLLECTION
© 1987 JILL BARKLEM

Back Stamp	*U.S. $*	*Can. $*	*U.K. £*	*Aust. $*
BH-1	75.00	100.00	35.00	75.00

DBH18
STORE STUMP MONEY BOX™

Designer: Martyn Alcock
Height: 3 1/4", 8.3 cm
Colour: Brown
Issued: 1987 to the present

Royal Doulton®
STORE STUMP MONEY BOX
DBH 18
FROM THE BRAMBLY HEDGE
GIFT COLLECTION
© 1987 JILL BARKLEM

Back Stamp	*U.S. $*	*Can. $*	*U.K. £*	*Aust. $*
BH-1	75.00	100.00	30.00	75.00

DBH19
LILY WEAVER™

Designer:	Graham Tongue
Modeller:	Ted Chawner
Height:	3 1/4", 8.3 cm
Colour:	White dress with green and mauve, white cap
Issued:	1988 - 1993

Back Stamp	*U.S. $*	*Price* *Can. $*	*U.K. £*	*Aust. $*
BH-1	22.50	40.00	30.00	75.00

DBH20
FLAX WEAVER™

Designer:	Graham Tongue
Modeller:	Ted Chawner
Height:	3 1/4", 8.3 cm
Colour:	Grey trousers, grey and white striped shirt
Issued:	1988 - 1993

Back Stamp	*U.S. $*	*Price* *Can. $*	*U.K. £*	*Aust. $*
BH-1	22.50	40.00	30.00	75.00

DBH21
CONKER™

Designer:	Graham Tongue
Modeller:	Ted Chawner
Height:	3 1/4", 8.3 cm
Colour:	Green jacket, yellow waistcoat, green striped trousers
Issued:	1988 - 1994

Back Stamp	*U.S. $*	*Price* *Can. $*	*U.K. £*	*Aust. $*
BH-1	40.00	52.00	25.00	64.00

DBH22
PRIMROSE ENTERTAINS™

Designer: Graham Tongue
Modeller: Alan Maslankowski
Height: 3 1/4", 8.3 cm
Colour: Green and yellow dress
Issued: 1991 to the present

Back Stamp	*U.S. $*	*Price Can. $*	*U.K. £*	*Aust. $*
BH-1	66.00	101.00	24.00	110.00

DBH23
WILFRID ENTERTAINS™

Designer: Graham Tongue
Modeller: Alan Maslankowski
Height: 3 1/4", 8.3 cm
Colour: Burgundy and yellow outfit, black hat
Issued: 1991 to the present

Back Stamp	*U.S. $*	*Price Can. $*	*U.K. £*	*Aust $*
BH-1	66.00	101.00	24.00	110.00

DBH24
MR. SALTAPPLE™

Designer: Graham Tongue
Modeller: Warren Platt
Height: 3 1/4", 8.3 cm
Colour: Blue and white striped outfit, beige base
Issued: 1993 to the present

Back Stamp	*U.S. $*	*Price Can. $*	*U.K. £*	*Aust. $*
BH-1	40.00	55.00	15.95	64.00

DBH25
MRS. SALTAPPLE™

Designer:	Graham Tongue
Modeller:	Warren Platt
Height:	3 1/4", 8.3 cm
Colour:	Rose and cream dress, beige hat and base
Issued:	1993 to the present

Back Stamp	*U.S. $*	*Price* *Can. $*	*U.K. £*	*Aust. $*
BH-1	40.00	55.00	15.95	64.00

DBH26
DUSTY AND BABY™

Designer:	Graham Tongue
Modeller:	Martyn C. R. Alcock
Height:	3 3/4", 9.5 cm
Colour:	Dusty wears a blue striped shirt with beige dungarees. The baby has a white gown
Issued:	1995 to the present

Back Stamp	*U.S. $*	*Price* *Can. $*	*U.K. £*	*Aust. $*
BH-1	40.00	55.00	15.95	64.00

BUNNYKINS

BUNNYKINS BACKSTAMPS

BK-1. DOULTON & CO. LIMITED: 1972-1976

Used on all figurines introduced between 1972 and 1976.

BK-2. ROYAL DOULTON TABLEWARE LTD: 1976-1984

The "Doulton & Co. Limited" was changed to "Royal Doulton Tableware Ltd." Used on all new figurines introduced between 1976 and 1984. This new backstamp was also on all models that had been in production previously updating the older backstamp (BK-1). In these instances the copyright year on the stamps was kept the same as that of the original backstamp (BK-1).

BK-3 GOLDEN JUBILEE CELEBRATION: 1984

All Models manufactured during 1984 carried the words Golden Jubilee Celebration 1984 which was added to the 1976-1984 backstamp (BK-2).

BK-4. ROYAL DOULTON (U.K.): 1985-1986

The backstamp of 1976-1984 was modified to "Royal Doulton (U.K.)". All items introduced between 1985 and 1986 carry this backstamp.

BK-5. ROYAL DOULTON: 1987 TO DATE

The backstamp of 1985-86 was again modified by removing the (U.K.). All new figurines introduced since 1987 carry this backstamp.

BK-SPECIALS. SPECIAL COMMISSION BACKSTAMPS

Many figurines are issued for special events, anniversaries, promotions etc. All these carry a special stamp.

BILLY BUNNYKINS™
D6001

Designer: Charles Noke
Height: 4 1/2", 11.4 cm
Colour: Brown bunny, red trousers blue jacket, white bow tie with blue spots
Issued: 1939-c.1940's

FARMER BUNNYKINS™
D6003

Designer: Charles Noke
Height: 7 1/2", 19 cm
Colour: Green, blue, brown, red and white
Issued: 1939-c.1940's

FREDDIE BUNNYKINS™
D6024

Designer: Charles Noke
Height: 3 3/4", 9.5 cm
Colour: Brown bunny, Green trousers red jacket and yellow bow tie
Issued: 1939-c.1940's

MARY BUNNYKINS™
D6002

Designer: Charles Noke
Height: 6 1/2", 16.5 cm
Colour: Brown bunny, blue and red dress with white apron
Issued: 1939-c.1940's

MOTHER BUNNYKINS™
D6004

Designer: Charles Noke
Height: 7", 17.5 cm
Colour: Blue, red, white and brown
Issued: 1939-c.1940's

REGGIE BUNNYKINS™
D6025

Designer: Charles Noke
Height: 3 3/4", 9.5 cm
Colour: Brown bunny, blue dress and red bow tie
Issued: 1939-c.1940's

Name	*Back Stamp*	*Doulton Number*	*Price* *U.S. $*	*Can. $*	*U.K. £*	*Aust. $*
Billy Bunnykins	BK-	D6001	3,200.00	3,500.00	2,000.00	3,000.00
Farmer Bunnykins	BK-	D6003	3,500.00	3,700.00	2,000.00	3,000.00
Freddie Bunnykins	BK-	D6024	4,000.00	4,250.00	2,250.00	3,000.00
Mary Bunnykins	BK-	D6002	3,500.00	3,700.00	2,000.00	3,000.00
Mother Bunnykins	BK-	D6004	3,500.00	3,700.00	2,000.00	3,000.00
Reggie Bunnykins	BK-	D6025	4,000.00	4,250.00	2,250.00	3,000.00

For illustration of the above mentioned figures see page 140.

D6615A
BUNNY BANK™
First Version

Designer:	Unknown
Modeller:	Unknown
Height:	8 1/2", 21.6 cm
Colour:	Grey rabbit, green coat and hat, maroon drum
Issued:	1967 - 1977

Back Stamp	Price U.S. $	Can. $	U.K. £	Aust. $
BK-	350.00	375.00	150.00	375.00

D6615B
BUNNY BANK™
Second Version

Designer:	Unknown
Modeller:	Unknown
Height:	9 1/4", 23.5 cm
Colour:	Brown rabbit, green coat and hat, maroon drum
Issued:	1979 - 1991

Back Stamp	*Price U.S. $*	*Can. $*	*U.K. £*	*Aust. $*
BK-	250.00	275.00	100.00	375.00

DB1
FAMILY PHOTOGRAPH BUNNYKINS ™
First Version

Designer: Walter Hayward
Modeller: Albert Hallam
Height: 4 1/2", 11.4 cm
Colour: Blue, white, burgundy and grey
Issued: 1972 - 1988 (© 1972)
Varieties: DB67

BUNNYKINS
"Family Photograph"
DB1
COPR 1972
DOULTON & CO. LIMITED
Rd. No. 956232
Rd. No. 12899
R.S.A. Rd. No. 189/72

Back Stamp	*U.S. $*	*Price Can. $*	*U.K. £*	*Aust. $*
BK-1	100.00	150.00	70.00	225.00
BK-2	100.00	150.00	70.00	225.00
BK-3	100.00	150.00	70.00	225.00

DB2
BUNTIE BUNNYKINS HELPING MOTHER™

Designer: Walter Hayward
Modeller: Albert Hallam
Height: 3 1/2", 8.9 cm
Colour: Rose-pink and yellow
Issued: 1972 - 1993 (© 1972)

BUNTIE BUNNYKINS
"Helping Mother"
DB2
COPR 1972
DOULTON & CO. LIMITED
Rd No 956234
Rd No 12900
R.S.A. Rd No 193/72

Back Stamp	*U.S. $*	*Price Can. $*	*U.K. £*	*Aust. $*
BK-1	60.00	75.00	25.00	85.00
BK-2	60.00	75.00	25.00	85.00
BK-3	60.00	75.00	25.00	85.00

DB3
BILLIE BUNNYKINS COOLING OFF™

Designer: Walter Hayward
Modeller: Albert Hallam
Height: 3 3/4", 9.5 cm
Colour: Burgundy, yellow and green-grey
Issued: 1972 - 1987 (© 1972)

BILLIE BUNNYKINS
"Cooling Off"
DB3
COPR 1972
DOULTON & CO. LIMITED
Rd. No. 956235
Rd. No. 12901

Back Stamp	*U.S. $*	*Price Can. $*	*U.K. £*	*Aust. $*
BK-1	150.00	175.00	150.00	225.00
BK-2	150.00	175.00	150.00	225.00
BK-3	150.00	175.00	150.00	225.00

DB4
BILLIE AND BUNTIE BUNNYKINS SLEIGH RIDE™
First Version

Designer:	Walter Hayward
Modeller:	Albert Hallam
Height:	3 1/4", 8.3 cm
Colour:	Blue, maroon and yellow
Issued:	1972 to the present (© 1972)
Varieties:	DB81

MADE IN ENGLAND
ROYAL DOULTON
ENGLAND
BILLIE & BUNTIE
BUNNYKINS
"Sleigh Ride"
DB4
© ROYAL DOULTON
TABLEWARE LTD 1972

Back Stamp	*U.S. $*	*Price Can. $*	*U.K. £*	*Aust. $*
BK-1	40.00	46.00	13.50	64.00
BK-2	40.00	46.00	13.50	64.00
BK-3	40.00	46.00	13.50	64.00

DB5
MR. BUNNYKINS AUTUMN DAYS™

Designer:	Walter Hayward
Modeller:	Albert Hallam
Height:	4', 10.1 cm
Colour:	Maroon, yellow and blue
Issued:	1972 - 1982 (© 1972)

MR. BUNNYKINS
"Autumn Days"
DB5
COPR 1972
DOULTON & CO LIMITED
Rd No 958236
Rd No 12903
R.S.A Rd No 192/72

Back Stamp	*U.S. $*	*Price Can. $*	*U.K. £*	*Aust. $*
BK-1	400.00	450.00	225.00	800.00
BK-2	400.00	450.00	225.00	800.00
BK-3	400.00	450.00	225.00	800.00

DB6
MRS. BUNNYKINS CLEAN SWEEP™

Designer:	Walter Hayward
Modeller:	Albert Hallam
Height:	4", 10.1 cm
Colour:	Blue and white
Issued:	1972 - 1991 (© 1972)

MRS. BUNNYKINS
"Clean Sweep"
DB6
COPR 1972
DOULTON & CO LIMITED
Rd No 956233
Rd No 12904
R.S.A Rd No 186/72

Back Stamp	*U.S. $*	*Price Can. $*	*U.K. £*	*Aust. $*
BK-1	75.00	95.00	40.00	70.00
BK-2	75.00	95.00	40.00	70.00
BK-3	75.00	95.00	40.00	70.00
BK-6	75.00	95.00	40.00	70.00

DB7
DAISIE BUNNYKINS SPRINGTIME™

Designer:	Walter Hayward
Modeller:	Albert Hallam
Height:	3 1/2", 8.9 cm
Colour:	Blue, white and yellow
Issued:	1972 - 1983 (© 1972)

Back Stamp	*U.S. $*	*Price Can.*	*U.K. £*	*Aust. $*
BK-1	475.00	525.00	275.00	1,000.00
BK-2	475.00	525.00	275.00	1,000.00
BK-3	475.00	525.00	275.00	1,000.00

DB8
DOLLIE BUNNYKINS PLAYTIME™

Designer:	Walter Hayward
Modeller:	Albert Hallam
Height:	4", 10.1 cm
Colour:	White dress with pink design; blue dress
Issued:	1972 - 1993 (© 1972)
Varieties:	DB80

Back Stamp	*U.S. $*	*Price Can. $*	*U.K. £*	*Aust. $*
BK-1	60.00	75.00	23.00	70.00
BK-2	60.00	75.00	23.00	70.00
BK-3	60.00	75.00	23.00	70.00

DB9
STORYTIME BUNNYKINS™
First Version

Designer:	Walter Hayward
Modeller:	Albert Hallam
Height:	3", 7.6 cm
Colour:	White dress with blue design; pink dress
Issued:	1972 to the present (© 1972)
Varieties:	DB59; Also called "Partners in Collecting" DB151

Back Stamp	*U.S. $*	*Price Can. $*	*U.K. £*	*Aust. $*
BK-1	40.00	46.00	13.50	70.00
BK-2	40.00	46.00	13.50	70.00
BK-3	40.00	46.00	13.50	70.00

DB10
BUSY NEEDLES BUNNYKINS™

Designer:	Walter Hayward
Modeller:	Albert Hallam
Height:	3 1/4", 8.3 cm
Colour:	White, green and maroon
Issued:	1973 - 1988 (©1974)
Varieties:	DB70

Back Stamp	*U.S. $*	*Price Can. $*	*U.K. £*	*Aust. $*
BK-1	75.00	110.00	65.00	225.00
BK-2	75.00	110.00	65.00	225.00
BK-3	75.00	110.00	65.00	225.00

DB11
RISE AND SHINE BUNNYKINS™

Designer:	Walter Hayward
Modeller:	Albert Hallam
Height:	3 3/4", 9.5 cm
Colour:	Maroon, yellow and blue
Issued:	1973 - 1988 (© 1974)

Back Stamp	*U.S. $*	*Price Can. $*	*U.K. £*	*Aust. $*
BK-1	140.00	175.00	95.00	225.00
BK-2	140.00	175.00	95.00	225.00
BK-3	140.00	175.00	95.00	225.00

DB12
TALLY HO! BUNNYKINS ™
First Version

Designer:	Walter Hayward
Modeller:	Albert Hallam
Height:	3 3/4", 9.5 cm
Colour:	Burgundy, yellow, blue, white and green
Issued:	1973 - 1988
Varieties:	DB78 (© 1974)

Back Stamp	*U.S. $*	*Price Can. $*	*U.K. £*	*Aust. $*
BK-1	90.00	125.00	45.00	225.00
BK-2	90.00	125.00	45.00	225.00
BK-3	90.00	125.00	45.00	225.00

DB13
THE ARTIST™

Designer:	Walter Hayward
Modeller:	Alan Maslankowski
Height:	3 3/4", 9.5 cm
Colour:	Burgundy, yellow and blue
Issued:	1974 - 1982 (© 1975)

Back Stamp	*U.S. $*	*Price Can. $*	*U.K. £*	*Aust. $*
BK-1	425.00	500.00	300.00	600.00
BK-2	425.00	500.00	300.00	600.00

DB14
GRANDPA'S STORY BUNNYKINS™

Designer:	Walter Hayward
Modeller:	Alan Maslankowski
Height:	4", 10.1 cm
Colour:	Burgundy, grey, yellow, blue and green
Issued:	1974 - 1983 (© 1975)

Back Stamp	*U.S. $*	*Price Can. $*	*U.K. £*	*Aust. $*
BK-1	350.00	400.00	300.00	800.00
BK-2	350.00	400.00	300.00	800.00

DB15
SLEEPYTIME™

Designer:	Walter Hayward
Modeller:	Alan Maslankowski
Height:	1 3/4", 4.7 cm
Colour:	Brown, white, yellow, blue and red
Issued:	1974 - 1993 (© 1975)

Back Stamp	*U.S. $*	*Price Can. $*	*U.K. £*	*Aust. $*
BK-1	60.00	70.00	20.00	75.00
BK-2	60.00	70.00	20.00	75.00
BK-3	60.00	70.00	20.00	75.00

DB16
MR. BUNNYBEAT STRUMMING™

Designer: Harry Sales
Modeller: David Lyttleton
Height: 4 1/2", 11.4 cm
Colour: Pink and yellow coat, blue and white striped trousers, white with blue polka-dot neck-bow
Issued: 1982 - 1988 (© 1981)

MR. BUNNYBEAT
Strumming
DB 16
© ROYAL DOULTON
TABLEWARE LTD 1981

Back		*Price*		
Stamp	***U.S. $***	***Can. $***	***U.K. £***	***Aust. $***
BK-2	175.00	200.00	90.00	200.00
BK-3	175.00	200.00	90.00	200.00

DB17
SANTA BUNNYKINS HAPPY CHRISTMAS™

Designer: Harry Sales
Modeller: David Lyttleton
Height: 4 1/2", 10.8 cm
Colour: Red, white and brown
Issued: 1981 to the present (© 1981)

SANTA BUNNYKINS
Happy Christmas
DB 17
© ROYAL DOULTON
TABLEWARE LTD 1981

Back		*Price*		
Stamp	***U.S. $***	***Can. $***	***U.K. £***	***Aust. $***
BK-2	40.00	55.00	16.95	59.00
BK-3	40.00	55.00	16.95	59.00

DB18
MR. BUNNYKINS AT THE EASTER PARADE ™
First Version

Designer: Harry Sales
Modeller: David Lyttleton
Height: 5", 12.7 cm
Colour: Red, yellow and brown
Issued: 1982 - 1993 (© 1982)
Varieties: DB 51

MR BUNNYKINS
At The Easter Parade
DB 18
© ROYAL DOULTON
TABLEWARE LTD 1982

Back		*Price*		
Stamp	***U.S. $***	***Can. $***	***U.K. £***	***Aust. $***
BK-2	60.00	75.00	25.00	75.00
BK-3	60.00	75.00	25.00	75.00

DB19
MRS. BUNNYKINS AT THE EASTER PARADE ™
First Version

Designer: Harry Sales
Modeller: David Lyttleton
Height: 4 1/2", 11.4 cm
Colour: Pale blue and maroon
Issued: 1982 to the present (© 1982)
Varieties: DB 52

MRS BUNNYKINS
"At The Easter Parade"
DB 19
© ROYAL DOULTON
TABLEWARE LTD 1982

Back Stamp	*Price U.S. $*	*Can. $*	*U.K. £*	*Aust. $*
BK-2	40.00	55.00	16.95	65.00
BK-3	40.00	55.00	16.95	65.00

DB20
ASTRO BUNNYKINS ROCKET MAN™

Designer: Harry Sales
Modeller: David Lyttleton
Height: 4 1/4", 10.8 cm
Colour: White, red, blue and yellow
Issued: 1983 - 1988 (© 1982)

ASTRO BUNNYKINS
Rocket Man
DB 20
ROYAL DOULTON
TABLEWARE LTD 1982

Back Stamp	*Price U.S. $*	*Can. $*	*U.K. £*	*Aust. $*
BK-2	125.00	140.00	55.00	100.00
BK-3	125.00	140.00	55.00	100.00

DB21
HAPPY BIRTHDAY BUNNYKINS™

Designer: Harry Sales
Modeller: Graham Tongue
Height: 3 3/4", 9.5 cm
Colour: Red and blue
Issued: 1983 to the present (© 1982)

BIRTHDAY BUNNYKINS"
DB 21
© ROYAL DOULTON
TABLEWARE LTD. 1982

Back Stamp	*Price U.S. $*	*Can. $*	*U.K. £*	*Aust. $*
BK-2	40.00	55.00	16.95	65.00
BK-3	40.00	55.00	16.95	65.00

DB22
JOGGING BUNNYKINS™

Designer:	Harry Sales
Modeller:	David Lyttleton
Height:	2 1/2", 6.4 cm
Colour:	Yellow, blue and white
Issued:	1983 - 1989 (© 1982)

"JOGGING BUNNYKINS"
DB22
© ROYAL DOULTON
TABLEWARE LTD 1982

Back Stamp	*Price* *U.S. $*	*Can. $*	*U.K. £*	*Aust. $*
BK-2	100.00	120.00	60.00	100.00
BK-3	100.00	120.00	60.00	100.00

DB23
SOUSAPHONE BUNNYKINS ™
First Version

Designer:	Harry Sales
Modeller:	David Lyttleton
Height:	3 1/2", 8.9 cm
Colour:	Red, blue and yellow
Issued:	1984 - 1990 (© 1983)
Varieties:	DB86, DB105
Series:	Bunnykins Oompah Band

"SOUSAPHONE BUNNYKINS"
FROM THE OOMPAH BAND
DB23
© ROYAL DOULTON
TABLEWARE LTD 1983
GOLDEN JUBILEE
CELEBRATION 1984

Back Stamp	*Price* *U.S. $*	*Can. $*	*U.K. £*	*Aust. $*
BK-3	125.00	140.00	65.00	95.00

DB24
TRUMPETER BUNNYKINS™
First Version

Designer:	Harry Sales
Modeller:	David Lyttleton
Height:	3 1/2', 8.9 cm
Colour:	Red, blue and yellow
Issued:	1984 - 1990
Varieties:	DB87, DB106
Series:	Bunnykins Oompah Band

"TRUMPETER BUNNYKINS"
FROM THE OOMPAH BAND
DB24
© ROYAL DOULTON
TABLEWARE LTD 1983
GOLDEN JUBILEE
CELEBRATION 1984

Back Stamp	*Price* *U.S. $*	*Can. $*	*U.K. £*	*Aust. $*
BK-3	100.00	120.00	65.00	95.00

DB25
CYMBALS BUNNYKINS™
First Version

Designer:	Harry Sales
Modeller:	David Lyttleton
Height:	3 1/2", 8.9 cm
Colour:	Red, blue and yellow
Issued:	1984 - 1990 (© 1972)
Varieties:	DB 88, DB 107
Series:	Bunnykins Oompah Band

"CYMBALS BUNNYKINS"
FROM THE OOMPAH BAND
DB 25
© ROYAL DOULTON
TABLEWARE LTD. 1983
GOLDEN JUBILEE
CELEBRATION 1984

Back		*Price*		
Stamp	*U.S. $*	*Can. $*	*U.K. £*	*Aust. $*
BK-3	100.00	120.00	55.00	95.00

DB26A
DRUMMER BUNNYKINS ™
Bunnykins Oompah Band Edition
First Version

Designer:	Harry Sales
Modeller:	David Lyttleton
Height:	3 3/4", 9.5 cm
Colour:	Blue, yellow, red and cream
Issued:	1984 - 1990 (© 1983)
Varieties:	DB 89, DB 108
Series:	Bunnykins Oompah Band

Back		*Price*		
Stamp	*U.S. $*	*Can. $*	*U.K £*	*Aust. $*
BK-3	135.00	150.00	55.00	110.00

DB26B
DRUMMER BUNNYKINS™
50th Anniversary Edition
Second Version

Designer:	Harry Sales
Modeller:	David Lyttleton
Height:	3 1/2", 9.2 cm
Colour:	Blue, yellow, red and cream
Issued:	1984 - 1990
Series:	Bunnykins Oompah Band

"DRUMMER BUNNYKINS"
FROM THE OOMPAH BAND
DB 26
© ROYAL DOULTON
TABLEWARE LTD 1983
GOLDEN JUBILEE
CELEBRATION 1984

Back		*Price*		
Stamp	*U.S. $*	*Can. $*	*U.K. £*	*Aust. $*
BK-3	175.00	150.00	70.00	120.00

DB27
DRUM-MAJOR BUNNYKINS™
First Version

Designer:	Harry Sales
Modeller:	David Lyttleton
Height:	3 1/2", 8.9 cm
Colour:	Red, blue and yellow
Issued:	1984 - 1990
Varieties:	DB 90, DB 109
Series:	Bunnykins Oompah Band

Back Stamp	*U.S. $*	*Price Can. $*	*U.K. £*	*Aust. $*
BK-3	100.00	120.00	55.00	95.00

DB28A
OLYMPIC BUNNYKINS™
First Version

Designer:	Harry Sales
Modeller:	David Lyttleton
Height:	3 3/4", 9.4 cm
Colour:	White and blue
Issued:	1984 - 1988

Back Stamp	*U.S. $*	*Price Can. $*	*U.K. £*	*Aust. $*
BK-3	115.00	125.00	50.00	100.00

DB28B
OLYMPIC BUNNYKINS ™
Second Version

Designer:	Harry Sales
Modeller:	David Lyttleton
Height:	3 1/2", 8.9 cm
Colour:	Gold and green
Issued:	1984 - 1984 (© 1983)

Note: Made exclusively for the Australian market.

Back Stamp	*U.S. $*	*Price Can. $*	*U.K. £*	*Aust. $*
BK-'Special"	250.00	275.00	120.00	300.00

DB29A
TOUCHDOWN BUNNYKINS ™
First Version

Designer:	Harry Sales
Modeller:	David Lyttleton
Height:	3 1/4", 8.3 cm
Colour:	Blue and white
Issued:	1985 - 1988
Varieties:	DB 96, DB 100

"TOUCHDOWN BUNNYKINS"
DB 29
© ROYAL DOULTON
TABLEWARE LTD 1984
GOLDEN JUBILEE
CELEBRATION 1984

Back		*Price*		
Stamp	*U.S. $*	*Can. $*	*U.K. £*	*Aust. $*
BK-4	90.00	115.00	65.00	100.00
BK-5	90.00	115.00	65.00	100.00

DB29B
TOUCHDOWN BUNNYKINS™
Boston College - Second Version

Designer:	Harry Sales
Modeller:	David Lyttleton
Height:	3 1/4", 8.3 cm
Colour:	Maroon and gold
Issued:	1985 in a limited edition of 50

Back		*Price*		
Stamp	*U.S. $*	*Can. $*	*U.K. £*	*Aust. $*
BK-'Special'	2,200.00	2,000.00	800.00	1,200.00

DB30
KNOCKOUT BUNNYKINS™

Designer:	Harry Sales
Modeller:	David Lyttleton
Height:	4", 10.1 cm
Colour:	Yellow, green and white
Issued:	1985 - 1988 © 1985

"KNOCKOUT BUNNYKINS"
DB 30
© ROYAL DOULTON
TABLEWARE LTD 1984

Back		*Price*		
Stamp	*U.S. $*	*Can. $*	*U.K. £*	*Aust. $*
BK-4	125.00	150.00	85.00	150.00
BK-5	125.00	150.00	85.00	150.00

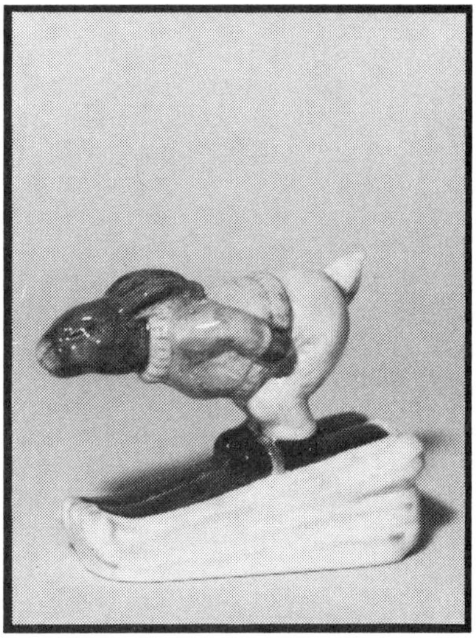

DB31
DOWNHILL BUNNYKINS™

Designer:	Harry Sales
Modeller:	Graham Tongue
Height:	2 1/2", 6.4 cm
Colour:	Yellow, green, maroon and grey
Issued:	1985 - 1988 (© 1984)

"DOWNHILL BUNNYKINS"
DB 31
© ROYAL DOULTON
TABLEWARE LTD 1984

Back Stamp	*U.S. $*	*Price Can. $*	*U.K. £*	*Aust. $*
BK-4	200.00	240.00	100.00	150.00
BK-5	200.00	240.00	100.00	150.00

DB32
BOGEY BUNNYKINS™

Designer:	Harry Sales
Modeller:	David Lyttleton
Height:	4", 10.1 cm
Colour:	Green, brown and yellow
Issued:	1985 - 1992 (© 1984)

"BOGEY BUNNYKINS"
DB 32
© ROYAL DOULTON
TABLEWARE LTD 1984

Back Stamp	*U.S. $*	*Price Can. $*	*U.K. £*	*Aust. $*
BK-4	100.00	125.00	60.00	100.00
BK-5	100.00	125.00	60.00	100.00

DB33A
TALLY HO!™
Music Box
First Version

Designer:	Walter Hayward
Modeller:	Albert Hallam
Height:	7", 17.8 cm
Colour:	Red coat, yellow jumper
Issued:	1984 - 1993 with "Tally Ho" figurine
Tune:	"Rock A Bye Baby"

Back Stamp	*U.S. $*	*Price Can. $*	*U.K. £*	*Aust. $*
BK-4	175.00	195.00	85.00	150.00
BK-5	175.00	195.00	85.00	150.00

DB33B
TALLY HO!™
Music Box
Second Version

Designer: Walter Hayward
Modeller: Albert Hallam
Height: 7", 17.8 cm
Colour: Brown trousers, red coat and maroon tie
Issued: 1988 - 1991 with "William" Bunnykins
Tune: "Rock A Bye Baby"

Back Stamp	*U.S. $*	*Price Can. $*	*U.K. £*	*Aust. $*
BK-4	275.00	250.00	85.00	125.00
BK-5	275.00	250.00	85.00	125.00

DB34
SANTA BUNNYKINS™
Music Box

Designer: Harry Sales
Modeller: David Lyttleton
Height: 7 1/4", 18.4 cm
Colour: Red, white and brown
Issued: 1984 - 1991
Tune: "White Christmas"

Back Stamp	*U.S. $*	*Price Can. $*	*U.K. £*	*Aust. $*
BK-4	175.00	195.00	85.00	125.00
BK-5	175.00	195.00	85.00	125.00

DB35
ASTRO BUNNYKINS ROCKET MAN™
Music Box

Designer: Harry Sales
Modeller: David Lyttleton
Height: 7", 17.8 cm
Colour: White, red and blue
Issued: 1984 - 1989
Tune: "Fly Me To The Moon"

Back Stamp	*U.S. $*	*Price Can. $*	*U.K. £*	*Aust. $*
BK-4	225.00	250.00	95.00	175.00
BK-5	225.00	250.00	95.00	175.00

DB36
HAPPY BIRTHDAY BUNNYKINS™
Music Box

Designer:	Harry Sales
Modeller:	Graham Tongue
Height:	7", 17.8 cm
Colour:	Red and white
Issued:	1984 - 1993
Tune:	"Happy Birthday To You"

Back Stamp	*U.S. $*	*Price Can. $*	*U.K. £*	*Aust. $*
BK-4	175.00	195.00	80.00	125.00
BK-5	175.00	195.00	80.00	125.00

DB37
JOGGING BUNNYKINS™
Music Box

Designer:	Harry Sales
Modeller:	David Lyttleton
Height:	5 1/2", 14.0 cm
Colour:	Yellow and blue
Issued:	1987 - 1989
Tune:	"King of the Road"

Back Stamp	*U.S. $*	*Price Can. $*	*U.K. £*	*Aust. $*
BK-5	300.00	350.00	100.00	175.00

DB38
MR. BUNNYBEAT STRUMMING ™
Music Box

Designer:	Harry Sales
Modeller:	David Lyttleton
Height:	7 1/2", 19.1 cm
Colour:	Pink, white and yellow
Issued:	1987 - 1989 (©1987)
Tune:	"Hey Jude"

Back Stamp	*U.S. $*	*Price Can. $*	*U.K. £*	*Aust. $*
BK-5	375.00	425.00	145.00	175.00

DB39
MRS. BUNNYKINS AT THE EASTER PARADE™
Music Box

Designer:	Harry Sales
Modeller:	David Lyttleton
Height:	7", 17.8 cm
Colour:	Blue, yellow and maroon
Issued:	1987 - 1991 (©1988)
Tune:	"Easter Parade"

Back Stamp	*Price* *U.S. $*	*Can. $*	*U.K. £*	*Aust. $*
BK-5	175.00	195.00	85.00	150.00

DB40
AEROBIC BUNNYKINS™

Designer:	Harry Sales
Modeller:	David Lyttleton
Height:	2 3/4", 7.0 cm
Colour:	Yellow and pale blue
Issued:	1985 - 1988 (© 1984)

"AEROBIC BUNNYKINS"
DB 40
© ROYAL DOULTON (UK) 1984

Back Stamp	*Price* *U.S. $*	*Can. $*	*U.K. £*	*Aust. $*
BK-4	175.00	195.00	85.00	150.00
BK-5	175.00	195.00	85.00	150.00

DB41
FREEFALL BUNNYKINS™

Designer:	Harry Sales
Modeller:	David Lyttleton
Height:	2 1/4", 5.7 cm
Colour:	Grey, yellow and white
Issued:	1986 - 1989 (© 1984)

"FREEFALL BUNNYKINS"
DB 41
© ROYAL DOULTON (UK) 1984

Back Stamp	*Price* *U.S. $*	*Can. $*	*U.K. £*	*Aust. $*
BK-4	225.00	275.00	150.00	150.00
BK-5	225.00	275.00	150.00	150.00

DB42
ACE BUNNYKINS™

Designer:	Harry Sales
Modeller:	David Lyttleton
Height:	3 3/4", 9.5 cm
Colour:	White and blue
Issued:	1986 - 1989 (© 1985)

MADE IN ENGLAND ROYAL DOULTON ENGLAND
ACE BUNNYKINS
DB 42
© ROYAL DOULTON (UK) 1985

Back Stamp	*Price U.S. $*	*Can. $*	*U.K. £*	*Aust. $*
BK-4	150.00	175.00	90.00	175.00
BK-5	150.00	175.00	90.00	175.00

DB43
HOME RUN BUNNYKINS™
(1 on back of jersey)

Designer:	Harry Sales
Modeller:	David Lyttleton
Height:	4", 10.1 cm
Colour:	Blue, yellow and white
Issued:	1986 - 1993 (© 1985)

MADE IN ENGLAND ROYAL DOULTON ENGLAND
HOME RUN BUNNYKINS
DB 43
© ROYAL DOULTON (UK) 1985

Back Stamp	*Price U.S. $*	*Can. $*	*U.K. £*	*Aust. $*
BK-4	75.00	95.00	25.00	100.00
BK-5	75.00	95.00	25.00	100.00

Note: The number DB 44 was assigned to the figurine "Ballet Bunnykins", however this figure was never issued.

DB45
KING JOHN™
First Version

Designer:	Harry Sales
Modeller:	David Lyttleton
Height:	4", 10.1 cm
Colour:	Red, yellow and blue
Issued:	1986 - 1990 (© 1985)
Varieties:	DB91
Series:	Bunnykins Royal Family

MADE IN ENGLAND ROYAL DOULTON ENGLAND
BUNNYKINS ROYAL FAMILY
KING JOHN
DB 45
© 1985 ROYAL DOULTON (UK)

Back Stamp	*Price U.S. $*	*Can. $*	*U.K. £*	*Aust. $*
BK-4	100.00	100.00	55.00	100.00
BK-5	100.00	100.00	55.00	100.00
Set DB45 - 49 (5 pcs.)	400.00	450.00	175.00	600.00

DB46
QUEEN SOPHIE™
First Version

Designer: Harry Sales
Modeller: David Lyttleton
Height: 4 1/2", 11.4 cm
Colour: Blue and red
Issued: 1986 - 1990 (© 1985)
Varieties: DB92
Series: Bunnykins Royal Family

Back Stamp	*U.S. $*	*Price Can. $*	*U.K. £*	*Aust. $*
BK-4	100.00	115.00	55.00	75.00
BK-5	100.00	115.00	55.00	75.00

DB47
PRINCESS BEATRICE™
First Version

Designer: Harry Sales
Modeller: David Lyttleton
Height: 3 1/2", 8.9 cm
Colour: Pale green
Issued: 1986 - 1990 (© 1985)
Varieties: DB93
Series: Bunnykins Royal Family

Back Stamp	*U.S. $*	*Price Can. $*	*U.K. £*	*Aust. $*
BK-4	85.00	100.00	45.00	75.00
BK-5	85.00	100.00	45.00	75.00

DB48
PRINCE FREDERICK™
First Version

Designer: Harry Sales
Modeller: David Lyttleton
Height: 3 1/2", 8.9 cm
Colour: Green, white and red
Issued: 1986 - 1990
Varieties: DB94
Series: Bunnykins Royal Family

Back Stamp	*U.S. $*	*Price Can. $*	*U.K. £*	*Aust. $*
BK-4	85.00	100.00	45.00	75.00
BK-5	85.00	100.00	45.00	75.00

DB49
HARRY THE HERALD™
First Version

Designer:	Harry Sales
Modeller:	David Lyttleton
Height:	3 1/2", 8.9 cm
Colour:	Maroon, white and tan
Issued:	1986 - 1990 (© 1985)
Varieties:	DB95, DB115
Series:	Bunnykins Royal Family

Back Stamp	*U.S. $*	*Price Can. $*	*U.K. £*	*Aust. $*
BK-4	100.00	125.00	80.00	75.00
BK-5	100.00	125.00	80.00	75.00

DB50
UNCLE SAM BUNNYKINS™

Designer:	Harry Sales
Modeller:	David Lyttleton
Height:	4 1/2", 11 cm
Colour:	Blue, red and white
Issued:	1986 to the present (© 1985)

Note: Made exclusively for the U.S. market

Back Stamp	*U.S. $*	*Price Can. $*	*U.K. £*	*Aust. $*
BK-4	40.00	60.00	30.00	100.00
BK-5	40.00	60.00	30.00	100.00

DB51
MR. BUNNYKINS AT THE EASTER PARADE ™
Second Version

Designer:	Harry Sales
Modeller:	David Lyttleton
Height:	5", 12.7 cm
Colour:	Blue tie and hat band, maroon coat, light grey trousers,pink ribbon on package
Issued:	1986 - 1986
Varieties:	DB18

Note: Made exclusively for distribution in the U.S. market at Beswick Artist Events

Back Stamp	*U.S. $*	*Price Can. $*	*U.K. £*	*Aust. $*
BK-'Special'	750.00	800.00	325.00	800.00

DB52
MRS. BUNNYKINS AT THE EASTER PARADE™
Second Version

Designer:	Harry Sales
Modeller:	David Lyttleton
Height:	4 1/2", 11.4 cm
Colour:	Maroon dress, white collar, blue bow on bonnet, multi-coloured bows on packages
Issued:	1986 - 1986
Varieties:	DB19

Note: Made exclusively for distribution in the U.S. market at Beswick Artist Events

Back Stamp	*U.S. $*	*Price Can. $*	*U.K. £*	*Aust. $*
BK-'Special'	850.00	900.00	375.00	800.00

DB53
CAROL SINGER™
Music Box

Designer:	Harry Sales
Modeller:	David Lyttleton
Height:	7", 17.8 cm
Colour:	Red, yellow and green
Issued:	1986 - 1989
Tune:	"Silent Night"

Back Stamp	*U.S. $*	*Price Can. $*	*U.K. £*	*Aust. $*
BK-4	275.00	150.00	100.00	175.00
BK-5	275.00	150.00	100.00	175.00

DB54
COLLECTOR BUNNYKINS™

Designer:	Harry Sales
Modeller:	David Lyttleton
Height:	4 1/4", 10.8 cm
Colour:	Brown, blue and grey
Issued:	1987 - 1987
Series:	R.D.I.C.C.

Back Stamp	*U.S. $*	*Price Can. $*	*U.K. £*	*Aust. $*
BK-'Special'	750.00	850.00	475.00	800.00

DB55
BEDTIME BUNNYKINS™
First Version

Designer:	Graham Tongue
Modeller:	David Lyttleton
Height:	3 1/4", 8.3 cm
Colour:	Blue and white striped pyjamas, brown teddy bear
Issued:	1987 to the present (© 1986)
Varieties:	DB63, 79, 103

Back Stamp	*Price U.S. $*	*Can. $*	*U.K. £*	*Aust. $*
BK-5	40.00	55.00	13.50	65.00

DB56
BE PREPARED BUNNYKINS™

Designer:	Graham Tongue
Modeller:	David Lyttleton
Height:	4", 10.1 cm
Colour:	Dark green and grey
Issued:	1987 to the present (© 1986)

Back Stamp	*Price U.S. $*	*Can. $*	*U.K. £*	*Aust. $*
BK-5	40.00	55.00	13.50	65.00

DB57
SCHOOL DAYS BUNNYKINS™

Designer:	Graham Tongue
Modeller:	David Lyttleton
Height:	3 1/2", 8.9 cm
Colour:	Dark green, white and yellow
Issued:	1987 -1995 (© 1986)

Back Stamp	*Price U.S. $*	*Can. $*	*U.K. £*	*Aust. $*
BK-5	50.00	55.00	13.50	65.00

DB58
AUSTRALIAN BUNNYKINS™

Designer:	Harry Sales
Modeller:	Warren Platt
Height:	4", 10.1 cm
Colour:	Gold and green
Issued:	1988 - 1988

Note: Sold exclusively in Australia celebrating the Australian Bicentenary

Back Stamp	*U.S. $*	*Price Can. $*	*U.K. £*	*Aust. $*
BK-'Special'	450.00	400.00	150.00	400.00

DB59
STORYTIME BUNNYKINS™
Second Version

Designer:	Walter Hayward
Modeller:	Albert Hallam
Height:	3", 7.6 cm
Colour:	Left: Green polka dots on white, yellow shoes Right: Yellow dress, green shoes
Issued:	1987 - 1987 (© 1974)
Varieties:	DB9; Also called "Partners in Collecting" DB151

Note: Produced for distribution at special events in the U.S.A.

Back Stamp	*U.S. $*	*Price Can. $*	*U.K. £*	*Aust. $*
BK-'Special'	400.00	425.00	110.00	150.00

DB60
SCHOOLMASTER BUNNYKINS™

Designer:	Graham Tongue
Modeller:	Warren Platt
Height:	4", 10 cm
Colour:	Black, white, green and white
Issued:	1987 to the present (© 1987)

Back Stamp	*U.S. $*	*Price Can. $*	*U.K. £*	*Aust. $*
BK-5	40.00	55.00	14.95	65.00

DB61
BROWNIE BUNNYKINS™

Designer: Graham Tongue
Modeller: Warren Platt
Height: 4", 10 cm
Colour: Brown uniform, yellow neck-tie
Issued: 1987 - 1993 (© 1987)

Back Stamp	*U.S. $*	*Price Can. $*	*U.K. £*	*Aust. $*
BK-5	50.00	50.00	20.00	75.00

DB62
SANTA BUNNYKINS HAPPY CHRISTMAS™
Christmas Tree Ornament

Designer: Harry Sales
Modeller: David Lyttleton
Height: Unknown
Colour: Red and white
Issued: 1987 in a limited edition of 1551

Back Stamp	*U.S. $*	*Price Can. $*	*U.K. £*	*Aust. $*
BK-"Special"	1,600.00	1,700.00	900.00	1,200.00

DB63
BEDTIME BUNNYKINS™
Second Version

Designer: Graham Tongue
Modeller: David Lyttleton
Height: 3 1/4", 8.3 cm
Colour: Red and white striped pyjamas, white teddy bear
Issued: 1987 - 1987 (© 1986)
Varieties: DB55, 79, 103

Note: Commissioned by D. H. Holmes, New Orleans, Louisiana

Back Stamp	*U.S. $*	*Price Can. $*	*U.K. £*	*Aust. $*
BK-'Special'	300.00	275.00	110.00	225.00

DB64
POLICEMAN BUNNYKINS™

Designer:	Graham Tongue
Modeller:	Martyn Alcock
Height:	4 1/4", 10.8 cm
Colour:	Dark blue uniform
Issued:	1988 to the present (© 1987)

Back Stamp	*U.S. $*	*Price* *Can. $*	*U.K. £*	*Aust. $*
BK-5	40.00	46.00	13.50	65.00

DB65
LOLLIPOPMAN BUNNYKINS™

Designer:	Graham Tongue
Modeller:	Martyn Alcock
Height:	3 3/4", 9.5 cm
Colour:	White and yellow
Issued:	1988 - 1991 (Reg'd 1987)

Back Stamp	*U.S. $*	*Price* *Can. $*	*U.K. £*	*Aust. $*
BK-5	65.00	90.00	60.00	85.00

DB66
SCHOOLBOY BUNNYKINS™

Designer:	Graham Tongue
Modeller:	Martyn Alcock
Height:	4", 10.1 cm
Colour:	Blue, white and grey
Issued:	1988 - 1991 (© 1987)

Back Stamp	*U.S. $*	*Price* *Can. $*	*U.K. £*	*Aust. $*
BK-5	50.00	65.00	25.00	85.00

DB67
FAMILY PHOTOGRAPH™
Second Version

Designer:	Walter Hayward
Modeller:	Albert Hallam
Height:	4 1/2", 11.4 cm
Colour:	Pink , black and white
Issued:	1988 - 1988 (©1972)
Varieties:	DB1

BUNNYKINS ®
"Family Photograph"
DB67
© 1972 ROYAL DOULTON
NEW COLOURWAY 1988
SPECIAL EVENTS – U.S.A. 1988

Note: New colourway produced in 1988 for Special Events in the U.S.A. 1988

Back Stamp	*Price U.S. $*	*Can. $*	*U.K. £*	*Aust. $*
BK-'Special'	225.00	195.00	85.00	150.00

DB68
FATHER, MOTHER AND VICTORIA BUNNYKINS™

Designer:	Based on design "Family Photograph" by Walter Hayward
Modeller:	Martyn Alcock
Height:	4 1/2", 11.4 cm
Colour:	Blue, grey, maroon and yellow
Issued:	1988 to the present (© 1988)

FATHER, MOTHER
& VICTORIA BUNNYKINS
DB 68
© 1988 ROYAL DOULTON

Back Stamp	*Price U.S. $*	*Can. $*	*U.K. £*	*Aust. $*
BK-5	40.00	55.00	14.95	65.00

DB69
WILLIAM BUNNYKINS™

Designer:	Based on design by Walter Hayward
Modeller:	Martyn Alcock
Height:	Unknown
Colour:	Red and white
Issued:	1988 - 1993

WILLIAM BUNNYKINS
DB 69
© 1988 ROYAL DOULTON

Back Stamp	*Price U.S. $*	*Can. $*	*U.K. £*	*Aust. $*
BK-5	65.00	75.00	20.00	75.00

DB70
SUSAN BUNNYKINS™

Designer:	Based on a design by Walter Hayward
Modeller:	Martyn Alcock
Height:	3 1/4", 8.3 cm
Colour:	White, blue and yellow
Issued:	1988 - 1993 (© 1988)

Back Stamp	*U.S. $*	*Price Can. $*	*U.K. £*	*Aust. $*
BK-5	60.00	75.00	20.00	75.00

DB71
POLLY BUNNYKINS™

Designer:	Graham Tongue
Modeller:	Martyn Alcock
Height:	3 1/2", 8.7 cm
Colour:	Pink
Issued:	1988 - 1993 (Reg'd 1988)

Back Stamp	*U.S. $*	*Price Can. $*	*U.K. £*	*Aust. $*
BK-5	60.00	75.00	20.00	75.00

DB72
TOM BUNNYKINS™

Designer:	Graham Tongue
Modeller:	Martyn Alcock
Height:	3", 7.6 cm
Colour:	Browns, white and blue
Issued:	1988 - 1993 (© 1988)

Back Stamp	*U.S. $*	*Price Can. $*	*U.K. £*	*Aust. $*
BK-5	60.00	75.00	20.00	75.00

DB73
HARRY BUNNYKINS™

Designer:	Graham Tongue
Modeller:	Martyn Alcock
Height:	3", 7.9 cm
Colour:	Blue, brown, white and yellow
Issued:	1988 - 1993 (© 1988)

Back Stamp	*U.S. $*	*Price Can. $*	*U.K. £*	*Aust. $*
BK-5	60.00	75.00	20.00	75.00

DB74A
NURSE BUNNYKINS™
First Version - Red Cross

Designer:	Graham Tongue
Modeller:	Martyn Alcock
Height:	4 1/4", 10.8 cm
Colour:	Dark and light blue and white, red cross.
Issued:	1989 - 1994 (© 1988)
Varieties:	DB 74B

Back Stamp	*U.S. $*	*Price Can. $*	*U.K. £*	*Aust. $*
BK-5	150.00	165.00	65.00	200.00

DB74B
NURSE BUNNYKINS™
Second Version - Green Cross

Designer:	Graham Tongue
Modeller:	Martyn Alcock
Height:	4 1/4", 10.8 cm
Colour:	Dark and light blue and white, green cross.
Issued:	1989 to the present (© 1988)
Varieties:	DB 74A

Back Stamp	*U.S. $*	*Price Can. $*	*U.K. £*	*Aust. $*
BK-5	40.00	65.00	13.95	65.00

DB75
FIREMAN BUNNYKINS™

Designer:	Graham Tongue
Modeller:	Martyn Alcock
Height:	4 1/4", 10.8 cm
Colour:	Dark blue and yellow
Issued:	1989 to the present (© 1988)

Back		*Price*		
Stamp	*U.S. $*	*Can. $*	*U.K. £*	*Aust. $*
BK-5	40.00	55.00	14.95	65.00

DB76
POSTMAN BUNNYKINS™

Designer:	Graham Tongue
Modeller:	Martyn Alcock
Height:	4 1/2", 11.4 cm
Colour:	Dark blue and red
Issued:	1989 - 1993 (© 1989)

Back		*Price*		
Stamp	*U.S. $*	*Can. $*	*U.K. £*	*Aust. $*
BK-5	50.00	50.00	35.00	90.00

DB77
PAPERBOY BUNNYKINS ™

Designer:	Graham Tongue
Modeller:	Martyn Alcock
Height:	4", 10.4 cm
Colour:	Green, yellow, red and white
Issued:	1989 - 1993

Back		*Price*		
Stamp	*U.S. $*	*Can. $*	*U.K. £*	*Aust. $*
BK-5	50.00	60.00	30.00	90.00

DB78
TALLY HO! BUNNYKINS™
Second Version

Designer:	Based on a design by Walter Hayward
Modeller:	Albert Hallam
Height:	4", 9.8 cm
Colour:	Light blue coat and white rocking horse, yellow sweater
Issued:	1988 - 1988 (© 1974)
Varieties:	DB12

Note: Commissioned by Macy's Department Store, New York, N.Y. Also painted in deeper shades of blue and yellow.

Back Stamp	*Price U.S. $*	*Can. $*	*U.K. £*	*Aust. $*
BK-'Special'	225.00	195.00	70.00	175.00

DB79
BEDTIME BUNNYKINS™
Third Version

Designer:	Graham Tongue
Modeller:	David Lyttleton
Height:	3 1/4", 8.3 cm
Colour:	Light blue and white
Issued:	1988 - 1988
Varieties:	DB55, 63, 103

Back Stamp	*Price U.S. $*	*Can. $*	*U.K. £*	*Aust. $*
BK-'Special'	275.00	300.00	180.00	125.00

DB80
DOLLIE BUNNYKINS PLAYTIME ™
Seccond Version

Designer:	Based on a design by Walter Hayward
Modeller:	Albert Hallam
Height:	4", 10.1 cm
Colour:	White and yellow
Issued:	1988 - 1988 (© 1972)
Varieties:	DB8

Note: Issued for the "Doulton Rooms" in the U.S.A. 250 in each edition

Back Stamp	*Type*	*Price U.S. $*	*Can. $*	*U.K. £*	*Aust. $*
BK-'Special'	"Higbee"	200.00	225.00	55.00	225.00
BK-'Special'	"Holmes "	200.00	225.00	55.00	225.00
BK-'Special'	"Hornes"	200.00	225.00	65.00	225.00
BK-'Special'	"Strawbridge"	200.00	225.00	55.00	225.00

DB81
BILLIE & BUNTIE BUNNYKINS SLEIGH RIDE™
Second Version

Designer: Based on a design by Walter Hayward
Modeller: Albert Hallam
Height: 3 1/2", 8.9 cm
Colour: Green, yellow and red
Issued: 1989 - 1989 (© 1972)
Varieties: DB4

Note: Special Events Tour 1989

Back Stamp	*U.S. $*	*Price Can. $*	*U.K. £*	*Aust. $*
Backstamp 'Special'	125.00	145.00	75.00	150.00

DB82
ICE CREAM BUNNYKINS™

Designer: Graham Tongue
Modeller: Warren Platt
Height: 4 1/2", 11.4 cm
Colour: White, blue and green
Issued: 1990 - 1993 (©1989)

ICE CREAM BUNNYKINS
DB 82
© 1989 ROYAL DOULTON

Back Stamp	*U.S. $*	*Price Can. $*	*U.K. £*	*Aust. $*
BK-5	90.00	100.00	40.00	90.00

DB83
SUSAN BUNNYKINS AS QUEEN OF THE MAY™

Designer: Graham Tongue
Modeller: Martyn Alcock
Height: 4", 10.2 cm
Colour: White polka dot dress, blue and brown chair
Issued: 1990 - 1991
© 1989

SUSAN BUNNYKINS
AS QUEEN OF THE MAY
DB 83
© 1989 ROYAL DOULTON

Back Stamp	*U.S. $*	*Price Can. $*	*U.K. £*	*Aust. $*
BK-5	90.00	100.00	35.00	90.00

DB84
FISHERMAN BUNNYKINS™

Designer:	Graham Tongue
Modeller:	Warren Platt
Height:	4 1/4", 10.8 cm
Colour:	Maroon, yellow and grey
Issued:	1990 - 1993 (© 1990)

FISHERMAN BUNNYKINS
DB 84
C 1990 ROYAL DOULTON

Back Stamp	*U.S. $*	*Price* *Can. $*	*U.K. £*	*Aust. $*
BK-5	100.00	120.00	40.00	90.00

DB85
COOK BUNNYKINS™

Designer:	Graham Tongue
Modeller:	Warren Platt
Height:	4 1/4", 10.8 cm
Colour:	White and green
Issued:	1990 - 1995 (© 1990)

COOK BUNNYKINS
DB 85
C 1990 ROYAL DOULTON

Back Stamp	*U.S. $*	*Price* *Can. $*	*U.K. £*	*Aust. $*
BK-5	60.00	44.00	13.50	90.00

DB86
SOUSAPHONE BUNNYKINS™
From the Oompah Band - Second Version

Designer:	Harry Sales
Modeller:	David Lyttleton
Height:	3 1/2", 8.9 cm
Colour:	Blue uniform and yellow sousaphone
Issued:	1990 in a limited edition of 250 sets (© 1990)
Series:	Royal Doulton Collectors Band
Varieties:	DB23, 105

SOUSAPHONE BUNNYKINS
FROM THE OOMPAH BAND
DB 86
© 1990 ROYAL DOULTON

Note: Special colourway edition of 250. Exclusive for U.K. Fairs Ltd.

Back Stamp	*U.S. $*	*Price* *Can. $*	*U.K. £*	*Aust. $*
BK-"U.K. Fairs"	200.00	225.00	100.00	300.00
DB86 to 90 (5 pcs.)	1,000.00	1,125.00	500.00	1,500.00

DB87
TRUMPETER BUNNYKINS™
From the Oompah Band - Second Version

Designer:	Harry Sales
Modeller:	David Lyttleton
Height:	3 3/4", 9.5 cm
Colour:	Blue uniform and yellow trumpet
Issued:	1990 in a limited edition of 250 sets
Series:	Royal Doulton Collectors Band
Varieties:	DB24, 106

"TRUMPETER BUNNYKINS"
FROM THE OOMPAH BAND
DB 87
© 1990 ROYAL DOULTON

Note: Special colourway edition of 250. Exclusive for U.K. Fairs Ltd.

Back Stamp	*U.S. $*	*Price Can. $*	*U.K. £*	*Aust. $*
BK-'Special'	200.00	225.00	100.00	300.00

DB88
CYMBALS BUNNYKINS™
From the Oompah Band - Second Version

Designer:	Harry Sales
Modeller:	David Lyttleton
Height:	3 1/2", 8.9 cm
Colour:	Blue uniform and yellow cymbals
Issued:	1990 in a limited edition of 250 sets
Series:	Royal Doulton Collectors Band
Varieties:	DB25, 107

"CYMBAL BUNNYKINS"
FROM THE OOMPAH BAND
DB 88
© 1990 ROYAL DOULTON

Note: Special colourway edition of 250. Exclusive for U.K. Fairs Ltd.

Back Stamp	*U.S. $*	*Price Can. $*	*U.K. £*	*Aust. $*
BK-'Special'	200.00	225.00	100.00	300.00

DB89
DRUMMER BUNNYKINS
Third Version

Designer:	Harry Sales
Modeller:	David Lyttleton
Height:	3 3/4", 9.5 cm
Colour:	Blue trousers and sleeves, yellow vest, cream and red drum
Issued:	1990 in a limited edition of 250 sets (© 1990)
Series:	Royal Doulton Collectors Band
Varieties:	DB26, 26A, 26B, 108

"DRUMMER BUNNYKINS"
FROM THE OOMPAH BAND
DB 89
SPECIAL COLOURWAY EDITION OF 250 SETS
EXCLUSIVE FOR UK FAIRS LTD.
© 1990 ROYAL DOULTON

Note: Special colourway edition of 250. Exclusive for U.K. Fairs Ltd.

Back Stamp	*U.S. $*	*Price Can. $*	*U.K. £*	*Aust. $*
BK-'Special'	200.00	225.00	100.00	300.00

DB90
DRUM-MAJOR BUNNYKINS™
Second Version

Designer:	Harry Sales
Modeller:	David Lyttleton
Height:	3 3/4", 9.5 cm
Colour:	Blue and yellow uniform
Issued:	1990 in a limited edition of 250 sets
Series:	Royal Doulton Collectors Band
Varieties:	DB27, 109

DRUM-MAJOR BUNNYKINS
FROM THE OOMPAH BAND
DB 90
© 1990 ROYAL DOULTON

Note: Special colourway edition of 250 Exclusive for U.K. Fairs Ltd.

Back Stamp	*Price U.S. $*	*Can. $*	*U.K. £*	*Aust. $*
BK-'Special'	200.00	225.00	100.00	350.00

DB91
KING JOHN™
Second Version

Designer:	Harry Sales
Modeller:	David Lyttleton
Height:	4", 10.1 cm
Colour:	Purple, yellow and white
Issued:	1990 in a limited edition of 250 sets (© 1990)
Series:	Bunnykins Royal Family
Varieties:	DB45

BUNNYKINS ROYAL FAMILY
KING JOHN
DB 91
EXCLUSIVE COLOURWAY OF 250 SETS
FOR UK I CERAMICS LTD
© 1990 ROYAL DOULTON

Note: Exclusive colourway of 250 sets for U.K. International Ceramics Ltd.

Back Stamp	*Price U.S. $*	*Can. $*	*U.K. £*	*Aust. $*
BK-'Special'	150.00	175.00	65.00	350.00
Set DB91 - 95 (5 Pcs)	400.00	500.00	250.00	1,750.00

DB92
QUEEN SOPHIE™
Second Version

Designer:	Harry Sales
Modeller:	David Lyttleton
Height:	4 1/2", 11.4 cm
Colour:	Pink and purple
Issued:	1990 in a limited edition of 250 (© 1990)
Series:	Bunnykins Royal Family
Varieties:	DB46

BUNNYKINS ROYAL FAMILY
QUEEN SOPHIE
DB 92
© 1990 ROYAL DOULTON

Note: Exclusive colourway of 250 sets. For U.K. International Ceramics Ltd.

Back Stamp	*Price U.S. $*	*Can. $*	*U.K. £*	*Aust. $*
BK-'Special'	150.00	175.00	65.00	350.00

DB93
PRINCESS BEATRICE™
Second Version

Designer:	Harry Sales
Modeller:	David Lyttleton
Height:	3 1/2", 8.9 cm
Colour:	Yellow and gold
Issued:	1990 in a limited edition of 250 (© 1990)
Series:	Bunnykins Royal Family
Varieties:	DB47

Note: Exclusive colourway of 250 sets. For U.K. International Ceramics Ltd.

Back Stamp	*Price* *U.S. $*	*Can. $*	*U.K. £*	*Aust. $*
BK-'Special'	150.00	175.00	65.00	350.00

DB94
PRINCE FREDERICK™
Second Version

Designer:	Harry Sales
Modeller:	David Lyttleton
Height:	3 1/2", 8.9 cm
Colour:	Red, blue and yellow
Issued:	1990 in a limited edition of 250 (© 1990)
Series:	Bunnykins Royal Family
Varieties:	DB48

Note: Exclusive colourway of 250 sets. For U.K. International Ceramics Ltd.

Back Stamp	*Price* *U.S. $*	*Can. $*	*U.K. £*	*Aust. $*
BK-'Special'	150.00	175.00	65.00	350.00

DB95
HARRY THE HERALD™
Second Version

Designer:	Harry Sales
Modeller:	David Lyttleton
Height:	3 1/2", 8.9 cm
Colour:	Blue, red and yellow
Issued:	1990 in a limited edition of 250 (© 1990)
Series:	Bunnykins Royal Family
Varieties:	DB49, 115

Note: Exclusive colourway of 250 sets. For U.K. International Ceramics Ltd.

Back Stamp	*Price* *U.S. $*	*Can. $*	*U.K. £*	*Aust. $*
BK-'Special'	150.00	175.00	85.00	350.00

DB96
TOUCHDOWN BUNNYKINS™
Ohio State University - Third Version

Designer:	Harry Sales
Modeller:	David Lyttleton
Height:	3 1/4", 8.3 cm
Colour:	Grey and orange
Issued:	1990 in a limited edition of 200
Varieties:	DB29, 29A, 29B, 97, 98, 99, 100

Note: Issued in a Limited Edition of 200

Back Stamp	*U.S. $*	*Price Can. $*	*U.K. £*	*Aust. $*
BK-'Special'	90.00	100.00	50.00	100.00
Set, DB96-100 (5 pcs)	400.00	500.00	225.00	500.00

DB97
TOUCHDOWN BUNNYKINS™
University of Michigan - Fourth Version

Designer:	Harry Sales
Modeller:	David Lyttleton
Height:	3 1/4", 8.3 cm
Colour:	Yellow and blue
Issued:	1990 in a limited edition of 200
Varieties:	DB29, 96, 98, 99, 100

Note: Issued in a Limited Edition of 200

Back Stamp	*U.S. $*	*Price Can. $*	*U.K. £*	*Aust. $*
BK-'Special'	90.00	100.00	50.00	100.00

DB98
TOUCHDOWN BUNNYKINS™
Cincinnati Bengals - Fifth Version

Designer:	Harry Sales
Modeller:	David Lyttleton
Height:	3 1/2", 8.3 cm
Colour:	Orange and black
Issued:	1990 (©1990)
Varieties:	DB29, 96, 97, 99, 100

Note: Issued in a Limited Edition of 200

Back Stamp	*U.S. $*	*Price Can. $*	*U.K. £*	*Aust. $*
BK-'Special'	90.00	100.00	50.00	100.00

DB99
TOUCHDOWN BUNNYKINS™
Notre Dame College - Sixth Version

Designer: Harry Sales
Modeller: David Lyttleton
Height: 3 1/2", 8.3 cm
Colour: Green and yellow
Issued: 1990 (©1990)
Varieties: DB29, 96, 97, 98, 100

Note: Issued in a Limited Edition of 200

Back Stamp	*U.S. $*	*Price Can. $*	*U.K. £*	*Aust. $*
BK-'Special'	200.00	225.00	65.00	400.00

DB100
TOUCHDOWN BUNNYKINS™
University of Indiana - Seventh Version

Designer: Harry Sales
Modeller: David Lyttleton
Height: 3 1/2", 8.3 cm
Colour: White and red
Issued: 1990 (©1990)
Varieties: DB29, 96, 97, 98, 99

Note: Issued in a Limited Edition of 200

Back Stamp	*U.S. $*	*Price Can. $*	*U.K. £*	*Aust. $*
BK-'Special'	200.00	225.00	65.00	400.00

DB101
BRIDE BUNNYKINS™

Designer: Graham Tongue
Modeller: Amanda Hughes-Lubeck
Height: 4", 10.1 cm
Colour: Cream dress, grey, blue and white train
Issued: 1991 to the present (©1990)

Back Stamp	*U.S. $*	*Price Can. $*	*U.K. £*	*Aust. $*
BK-5	40.00	62.00	16.95	64.00

DB102
GROOM BUNNYKINS™

Designer:	Graham Tongue
Modeller:	Martyn Alcock
Height:	4 1/2", 11.4 cm
Colour:	Grey and burgundy
Issued:	1991 to the present (©1990)

Back		*Price*		
Stamp	***U.S. $***	***Can. $***	***U.K. £***	***Aust. $***
BK-5	40.00	62.00	16.95	64.00

DB103
BEDTIME BUNNYKINS™
Fourth Version

Designer:	Graham Tongue
Modeller:	David Lyttleton
Height:	3 1/4", 8.3 cm
Colour:	Yellow and green striped pyjamas, brown teddy bear
Issued:	1991 - 1991 (©1986)
Varieties:	DB55, 63, 79

Note: U.S. Special Events Tour 1991

Back			*Price*		
Stamp	***Type***	***U.S. $***	***Can. $***	***U.K. £***	***Aust. $***
BK-'Special'	Pale Yellow	200.00	225.00	75.00	135.00
BK-'Special'	Daffodil Yellow	200.00	225.00	75.00	135.00

DB104
CAROL SINGER BUNNYKINS™

Designer:	Harry Sales
Modeller:	David Lyttleton
Height:	4", 10.1 cm
Colour:	Dark green, red, yellow and white
Issued:	1991 (© 1986)

Note: Special edition of 1000. Exclusive U.K. International Ceramics Ltd. 300 of edition have U.S.A. on backstamp

Back		*Price*		
Stamp	***U.S. $***	***Can. $***	***U.K. £***	***Aust. $***
BK-'Special'	200.00	215.00	45.00	110.00

DB105
SOUSAPHONE BUNNYKINS™
From the Oompah Band - Third Version

Designer:	Harry Sales
Modeller:	David Lyttleton
Height:	4", 10.1 cm
Colour:	Dark green, red and yellow
Issued:	1991 (© 1991)
Series:	Royal Doulton Collectors Band
Varieties:	DB 23, 86

Note: Issued in a Special Edition of 250 exclusive to U.K. Int'l Ceramics Ltd.

Back Stamp	*Price U.S. $*	*Can. $*	*U.K. £*	*Aust. $*
BK-'Special'	200.00	225.00	60.00	350.00
Set DB 105 to 109 5 pcs.	1,000.00	1,100.00	300.00	1,750.00

DB106
TRUMPETER BUNNYKINS™
From the Oompah Band - Third Version

Designer:	Harry Sales
Modeller:	David Lyttleton
Height:	3 3/4", 9.5 cm
Colour:	Dark green, red and yellow
Issued:	1991 (© 1991)
Series:	Royal Doulton Collectors Band
Varieties:	DB 24, 87

Note: Issued in a Special Edition of 250 exclusive to U.K. Int'l Ceramics Ltd.

Back Stamp	*Price U.S. $*	*Can. $*	*U.K. £*	*Aust. $*
BK-'Special'	200.00	225.00	60.00	350.00

DB107
CYMBALS BUNNYKINS™
From the Oompah Band - Third Version

Designer:	Harry Sales
Modeller:	David Lyttleton
Height:	4", 10.1 cm
Colour:	Dark green, red and yellow
Issued:	1991 (© 1991)
Series:	Royal Doulton Collectors Band
Varieties:	DB 25, 88

Note: Issued in a Special Edition of 250 exclusive to U.K. Int'l Ceramics Ltd.

Back Stamp	*Price U.S. $*	*Can. $*	*U.K. £*	*Aust. $*
BK-'Special'	200.00	225.00	60.00	350.00

DB 108
DRUMMER BUNNYKINS™
Fourth Version

Designer:	Harry Sales
Modeller:	David Lyttleton
Height:	3 1/2", 8.9 cm
Colour:	Dark green, red and white
Issued:	1991 (© 1991)
Series:	Royal Doulton Collectors Band
Varieties:	DB 26, 26A, 26B, 89

"DRUMMER BUNNYKINS"
FROM THE OOMPAH BAND
DB 108
SPECIAL COLOURWAY EDITION OF 250 SETS
EXCLUSIVE FOR U.K. FAIRS LTD.
© 1991 ROYAL DOULTON

Note: Special colourway edition of 250. Exclusive to U.K. Fairs Ltd.

Back Stamp	*U.S. $*	*Price Can. $*	*U.K. £*	*Aust. $*
BK-'Special'	200.00	225.00	60.00	350.00

DB 109
DRUM-MAJOR BUNNYKINS™
From the Oompah Band - Third Version

Designer:	Harry Sales
Modeller:	David Lyttleton
Height:	3 1/2", 8.9 cm
Colour:	Dark green, red and yellow
Issued:	1991 (© 1991)
Series:	Royal Doulton Collectors Band
Varieties:	DB 27, 90

DRUM-MAJOR BUNNYKINS
FROM THE OOMPAH BAND
DB 109
© 1991 ROYAL DOULTON

Note: Special colourway edition of 250. Exclusive to U.K. Int'l Ceramics Ltd

Back Stamp	*U.S. $*	*Price Can. $*	*U.K. £*	*Aust. $*
BK-'Special'	200.00	225.00	60.00	350.00

Note: DB 110 to 114 not issued

DB115
HARRY THE HERALD™
Third Version

Designer:	Harry Sales
Modeller:	David Lyttleton
Height:	3 1/2", 8.9 cm
Colour:	Yellow and dark blue
Issued:	1991
Series:	Bunnykins Royal Family
Varieties:	DB 49, 95

The International Doulton Collectors Weekend - A Special Edition of 300
BUNNYKINS ROYAL FAMILY
HARRY THE HERALD
DB 115
© 1985 ROYAL DOULTON

Note: Commissioned by Lambeth Productions in a special edition of 300.

Back Stamp	*U.S. $*	*Price Can. $*	*U.K. £*	*Aust. $*
BK-'Special'	300.00	400.00	300.00	350.00

DB116
GOALKEEPER BUNNYKINS ™
First Version

Designer:	Denise Andrews
Modeller:	Warren Platt
Height:	4 1/2", 11.4 cm
Colour:	Green and black
Issued:	1991 (© 1991)
Series:	Footballers
Varieties:	DB 118, 120, 122

Note: Exclusive to U.K. International Ceramics Ltd. Special edition of 250

Back Stamp	*U.S. $*	*Price Can. $*	*U.K. £*	*Aust. $*
BK-'Special'	150.00	200.00	110.00	350.00

DB117
FOOTBALLER BUNNYKINS™
First Version

Designer:	Denise Andrews
Modeller:	Warren Platt
Height:	4 1/2", 11.4 cm
Colour:	Green and white
Issued:	1991 (© 1991)
Series:	Footballers
Varieties:	DB 119, 121; Also called "Soccer Player" DB123

Note: Exclusive to U.K. International Ceramics Ltd. Special edition of 250

Back Stamp	*U.S. $*	*Price Can. $*	*U.K. £*	*Aust. $*
BK-'Special	150.00	200.00	110.00	350.00

DB118
GOALKEEPER BUNNYKINS ™
Second Version

Designer:	Denise Andrews
Modeller:	Warren Platt
Height:	4 1/2", 11.4 cm
Colour:	Red and black
Issued:	1991 (© 1991)
Series:	Footballers
Varieties:	DB 116, 120, 122

Note: Exclusive to U.K. International Ceramics Ltd. Special edition of 250

Back Stamp	*U.S. $*	*Price Can. $*	*U.K. £*	*Aust. $*
BK-'Special'	150.00	200.00	110.00	350.00

DB119
FOOTBALLER BUNNYKINS ™
Second Version

FOOTBALLER BUNNYKINS
DB 119
© 1991 ROYAL DOULTON
EXCLUSIVELY PRODUCED FOR
U.K. INTERNATIONAL CERAMICS LTD
SPECIAL EDITION OF 250 SETS

Designer:	Denise Andrews
Modeller:	Warren Platt
Height:	4 1/2", 11.4 cm
Colour:	Red
Issued:	1991 (© 1991)
Series:	Footballers
Varieties:	DB 117, 121; Also called "Soccer Player" DB123

Note: Exclusive to U.K. International Ceramics Ltd. Special edition of 250

Back Stamp	*Price U.S. $*	*Can. $*	*U.K. £*	*Aust. $*
BK-'Special'	150.00	200.00	110.00	350.00

DB120
GOALKEEPER BUNNYKINS ™
Third Version

GOALKEEPER BUNNYKINS
DB 120
© 1991 ROYAL DOULTON
EXCLUSIVELY PRODUCED FOR
U.K. INTERNATIONAL CERAMICS LTD
SPECIAL DOULTON FAIR EDITION
OF 250 SETS

Designer:	Denise Andrews
Modeller:	Warren Platt
Height:	4 1/2", 11.4 cm
Colour:	Yellow and black
Issued:	1991 (© 1991)
Series:	Footballers
Varieties:	DB 116, 118, 122

Note: Exclusive to U.K. International Ceramics Ltd. Special edition of 250

Back Stamp	*Price U.S. $*	*Can. $*	*U.K. £*	*Aust. $*
BK-'Special'	150.00	200.00	110.00	350.00

DB121
FOOTBALLER BUNNYKINS ™
Third Version

FOOTBALLER BUNNYKINS
DB 121
© 1991 ROYAL DOULTON
EXCLUSIVELY PRODUCED FOR
U.K. INTERNATIONAL CERAMICS LTD
SPECIAL DOULTON FAIR EDITION
OF 250 SETS

Designer:	Denise Andrews
Modeller:	Warren Platt
Height:	4 1/2", 11.4 cm
Colour:	White and blue
Issued:	1991 (© 1991)
Series:	Footballers
Varieties:	DB 117, 119; Also called "Soccer Player" DB123

Note: Exclusive to U.K. International Ceramics Ltd. Special edition of 250 sets

Back Stamp	*Price U.S. $*	*Can. $*	*U.K. £*	*Aust. $*
BK-'Special'	150.00	200.00	110.00	350.00

DB122
GOALKEEPER BUNNYKINS ™
Fourth Version

Designer:	Denise Andrews
Modeller:	Warren Platt
Height:	4 1/2", 1.4 cm
Colour:	Grey and black
Issued:	1991 (©1991)
Series:	Footballers
Varieties:	DB 118, 118, 120

Note: Exclusive to U.K. International Ceramics Ltd. Special edition of 250

Back Stamp	*U.S. $*	*Price Can. $*	*U.K. £*	*Aust. $*
BK-'Special'	150.00	200.00	110.00	350.00

DB123
SOCCER PLAYER BUNNYKINS ™

Designer:	Denise Andrews
Modeller:	Warren Platt
Height:	4 1/2", 11.4 cm
Colour:	Dark blue and white
Issued:	1991 (© 1991)
Series:	Footballers
Varieties:	DB 117, 119, 121

Note: Exclusive to U.K. International Ceramics Ltd. Special edition of 250 sets

Bacl Stamp	*U.S. $*	*Price Can. $*	*U.K. £*	*Aust. $*
BK-'Special'	150.00	200.00	110.00	350.00

DB124
ROCK 'N' ROLL BUNNYKINS™

Designer:	Harry Sales
Modeller:	David Lyttleton
Height:	4 1/2", 11.4 cm
Colour:	White, blue and red
Issued:	1991 (© 1991)

Note: Produced exclusively for Royal Doulton U.S.A. and Rock and Roll Hall of Fame, Cleveland. Limited Edition of 1000

Back Stamp	*U.S. $*	*Price Can. $*	*U.K. £*	*Aust. $*
BK-'Special'	225.00	250.00	85.00	200.00

Royal Doulton News

Marine City, MI, 1995

Beatrix Potter and Bunnykins - A Specialty At *Seaway China*

...When you have a store full of Royal Doulton - from the front door to the back room -- you have room for a lot of little characters. These little characters are of course the little characters from those world famous Beatrix Potter stories.

At Seaway China they have a very special home that they share with one of worlds largest collections of Bunnykins.

The gang at Seaway China pay special attention to all the old, current and recent releases of both Beatrix Potter and Bunnykins.

When you wish to add to your collection, give the gang at Seaway China a call. You can reach them from anywhere in the United States or Canada at 1-800-968-2424.

Seaway accepts all major credit cards and can usually ship orders the same day.

Michael Doulton is shown during his 1995 visit to Seaway China. With Michael are Dianne Goedkoop (R.D.I.C.C.) and singer Larry Burda.

Santa Tiny 1994 - Santa Tiny 1993

SERIES OF FOUR

Third Santa Tiny Ready for 1995.

Marine City, USA

Seaway China of Marine City, Michigan have announced that their third Santa Claus Tiny will be ready for the 1995 Christmas season.

Shown above are the first in the series (1993) with a red handle and the second (1994) with a red & white candy cane handle.

The series will contain four Santas.

Seaway China is accepting orders for these Character Jugs at 1-800-968-2424.

Shown above are a collection of Bunnykins at Seaway China. Call Seaway China at 1-800-968-2424 for more information about Bunnykins.

DB125
MILKMAN BUNNYKINS™

Designer: Graham Tongue
Modeller: Amanda Hughes-Lubeck
Height: 4 1/2", 11.4 cm
Colour: White, green and grey
Issued: 1992 (© 1991)

MILKMAN BUNNYKINS
DB 125
© 1991 ROYAL DOULTON
EXCLUSIVELY PRODUCED FOR
U.K. INTERNATIONAL CERAMICS LTD
SPECIAL EDITION OF 1,000 PIECES

Note: Commissioned by U.K. International Ceramics Ltd. in a special edition of 1,000.

Back Stamp	*U.S. $*	*Price Can. $*	*U.K. £*	*Aust. $*
BK-'Special'	250.00	225.00	45.00	200.00

DB126
MAGICIAN BUNNYKINS™

Designer: Graham Tongue
Modeller: Warren Platt
Height: 4 1/2", 11.4 cm
Colour: Black and yellow
Issued: 1992 (© 1992)

MAGICIAN BUNNYKINS
DB 126
© 1992 ROYAL DOULTON

Note: Commissioned by Pascoe & Co. and Charles Dombeck

Back Stamp	*U.S. $*	*Price Can. $*	*U.K. £*	*Aust. $*
BK-'Special'	150.00	175.00	65.00	200.00

DB127
GUARDSMAN BUNNYKINS™

Designer: Denise Andrews
Modeller: Warren Platt
Height: 4 1/2", 11.4 cm
Colour: Scarlet jacket, black trousers and bearskin hat
Issued: 1992 (© 1992)

GUARDSMAN BUNNYKINS
DB 127
PRODUCED EXCLUSIVELY
FOR U.K.I. CERAMICS LTD
IN A SPECIAL EDITION OF 1,000
© 1992 ROYAL DOULTON

Note: Produced exclusively for U.K.I. Ceramics Ltd. in a special edition of 1,000.

Back Stamp	*U.S. $*	*Price Can. $*	*U.K. £*	*Aust. $*
BK-'Special'	150.00	175.00	45.00	200.00

DB128
CLOWN BUNNYKINS™
First Version

Designer:	Denise Andrews
Modeller:	Warren Platt
Height:	4 1/4", 10.8 cm
Colour:	White costume with black patterned costume, red square on trousers and red ruff at neck
Issued:	1992 (© 1992)
Varieties:	DB 129

Note: Produced exclusively for U.K.I. Ceramics Ltd. in a special edition of 750

Back Stamp	*U.S. $*	*Price Can. $*	*U.K. £*	*Aust. $*
BK-'Special'	450.00	500.00	250.00	350.00

DB129
CLOWN BUNNYKINS™
Second Version

Designer:	Denise Andrews
Modeller:	Warren Platt
Height:	4 1/4", 10.8 cm
Colour:	White costume with red patterned costume, black ruff around neck
Issued:	1992 (© 1992)
Varieties:	DB 128

Note: Produced exclusively for U.K.I. Ceramics Ltd. in a special edition of 250.

Back Stamp	*U.S. $*	*Price Can. $*	*U.K. £*	*Aust. $*
BK-'Special'	1,500.00	1,500.00	500.00	800.00

DB130
SWEETHEART BUNNYKINS™

Designer:	Graham Tongue
Modeller:	Warren Platt
Height:	3 3/4", 9.5 cm
Colour:	Yellow sweater, blue trousers, red heart
Issued:	1992 to the present (© 1992)

Note: Introduced at the International Collectables Exposition at South Bend, Indiana, July 1992

Back Stamp	*U.S. $*	*Price Can. $*	*U.K. £*	*Aust. $*
BK-5	40.00	55.00	13.95	65.00

DB131
MASTER POTTER BUNNYKINS™

Designer:	Graham Tongue
Modeller:	Warren Platt
Height:	3 3/4", 9.3 cm
Colour:	Blue, white, green and brown
Issued:	1993 - 1993 (© 1992)
Series:	RDICC

INTERNATIONAL COLLECTORS CLUB ROYAL DOULTON
MASTER POTTER BUNNYKINS
DB 131
EXCLUSIVELY FOR
COLLECTORS CLUB
© 1992 ROYAL DOULTON

Note: Produced exclusively for the Royal Doulton International Collectors Club in 1993

Back Stamp	*U.S. $*	*Price* *Can. $*	*U.K. £*	*Aust. $*
BK-'Special'	175.00	160.00	65.00	135.00

DB132
HALLOWEEN BUNNYKINS™

Designer:	Graham Tongue
Modeller:	Martyn Alcock
Height:	3 1/4", 8.3 cm
Colour:	Orange and yellow pumpkin
Issued:	1993 to the present (© 1993)

HALLOWEEN BUNNYKINS
DB 132
© 1993 ROYAL DOULTON

Note: Pre-released in U.S.A. in 1993

Back Stamp	*U.S. $*	*Price* *Can.$*	*U.K. £*	*Aust. $*
BK-5	50.00	74.00	20.00	65.00

DB133
AUSSIE SURFER BUNNYKINS™

Designer:	Graham Tongue
Modeller:	Martyn Alcock
Height:	4", 10.1 cm
Colour:	Gold and green outfit, white and blue base
Issued:	1994 - 1994

AUSSIE SURFER
BUNNYKINS
DB 133
© 1993 ROYAL DOULTON
PRODUCED EXCLUSIVELY
FOR ROYAL DOULTON AUSTRALIA

Note: Produced exclusively for Royal Doulton, Australia

Back Stamp	*U.S. $*	*Price* *Can. $*	*U.K. £*	*Aust. $*
BK-'Special'	100.00	125.00	60.00	79.00

DB134
JOHN BULL BUNNYKINS™

Designer:	Denise Andrews
Modeller:	Amanda Hughes-Lubeck
Height:	4 1/2", 11 cm
Colour:	Grey, yellow, red, white and blue Union Jack waistcoat
Issued:	1993 (© 1993)

Note: Produced exclusively for U.K. International Ceramics Ltd. in a Special Limited Edition of 1,000

Back Stamp	*U.S. $*	*Price* *Can. $*	*U.K. £*	*Aust. $*
BK-'Special'	150.00	100.00	55.00	200.00

DB135
CONSTABLE MOUNTIE BUNNYKINS™

Designer:	Graham Tongue
Modeller:	Warren Platt
Height:	4", 10.1 cm
Colour:	Red jacket, dark blue trousers and brown hat
Issued:	1993 (© 1993)

Note: Produced exclusively for the Doulton Collectors Weekend in Toronto during 1993 in a special edition of 750. "1873-1993 120 Years"

Back Stamp	*U.S. $*	*Price* *Can. $*	*U.K. £*	*Aust. $*
BK-'Special'	300.00	350.00	160.00	650.00

DB136
SERGEANT MOUNTIE BUNNYKINS™

Designer:	Graham Tongue
Modeller:	Warren Platt
Height:	4", 10.1 cm
Colour:	Red jacket, dark blue trouser, brown hat and yellow stripes
Issued:	1993 (© 1993)

Note: Produced exclusively for the Doulton Collectors Weekend in Toronto during 1993 in a special edition of 250. "1873-1993 120 Years"

Back Stamp	*U.S. $*	*Price* *Can. $*	*U.K. £*	*Aust. $*
BK-'Special'	1,000.00	1,250.00	500.00	1,000.00

DB137
60TH ANNIVERSARY BUNNYKINS™

Designer: Denise Andrews
Modeller: Warren Platt
Height: 4 1/2", 11 cm
Colour: Lemon, yellow and white
Issued: 1994 - 1994

60th ANNIVERSARY
BUNNYKINS
DB 137
© 1993 ROYAL DOULTON

Back Stamp	U.S. $	Price Can. $	U.K. £	Aust. $
BK-6	60.00	75.00	25.00	65.00

DB142
CHEERLEADER BUNNYKINS™

Designer: Denise Andrews
Modeller: Warren Platt
Height: 4 1/2", 11 cm
Colour: Red
Issued: 1994 - 1994

CHEERLEADER BUNNYKINS
DB 142
PRODUCED EXCLUSIVELY
FOR U K I CERAMICS LTD
IN A SPECIAL EDITION OF 1,000
© 1994 ROYAL DOULTON
1994

Note: Produced exclusively for U.K. I. Ceramics Ltd. in a special edition of 1,000

Back Stamp	U.S. $	Price Can. $	U.K. £	Aust. $
BK-'Special'	125.00	150.00	38.00	250.00

DB143
CHEERLEADER BUNNYKINS™

Designer: Denise Andrews
Modeller: Warren Platt
Height: 4 1/2", 11 cm
Colour: Yellow
Issued: 1994 - 1994

CHEERLEADER BUNNYKINS
DB 143
PRODUCED EXCLUSIVELY
FOR U.K I CERAMICS LTD
DOULTON FAIRS
SPECIAL EDITION OF 1,000
© 1994 ROYAL DOULTON
1994

Note: Produced exclusivley for U.K. I. Ceramics Ltd. in a special edition of 1, 000 for Doulton Fairs in England

Back Stamp	U.S. $	Price Can. $	U.K. £	Aust. $
BK-'Special'	125.00	150.00	40.00	250.00

DB144
BATSMAN BUNNYKINS™

Designer: Denise Andrews
Modeller: Amanda Hughes-Lubeck
Height: 4", 10.1 cm
Colour: White, beige and black
Issued: 1994 - 1994

Note: Produced exclusively for U.K. I. Ceramics Ltd. in a special edition of 1,000

Back Stamp	U.S. $	Price Can. $	U.K. £	Aust. $
BK-'Special'	125.00	150.00	38.00	250.00

DB145
BOWLER BUNNYKINS™

Designer: Denise Andrews
Modeller: Warren Platt
Height: 4", 10.1 cm
Colour: White, beige and black
Issued: 1994 - 1994

BOWLER BUNNYKINS
DB 145
PRODUCED EXCLUSIVELY
FOR U.K I CERAMICS LTD
IN A SPECIAL EDITION OF 1,000
© 1994 ROYAL DOULTON
1994

Note: Produced exclusively for U.K. I. Ceramics Ltd. in a special edition of 1,000

Back Stamp	U.S. $	Price Can. $	U.K. £	Aust. $
BK-'Special'	125.00	150.00	38.00	250.00

DB146
CHRISTMAS SURPRISE BUNNYKINS™

Designer: Graham Tongue
Modeller: Warren Platt
Height: 3 1/2", 8.9 cm
Colour: Cream and Red
Issued: 1994 to the present

CHRISTMAS SURPRISE
BUNNYKINS
DB 146
© 1994 ROYAL DOULTON

Back Stamp	U.S. $	Price Can. $	U.K. £	Aust. $
BK-6	50.00	74.00	14.95	79.00

DB147
RAINYDAY BUNNYKINS™

Designer:	Graham Tongue
Modeller:	Warren Platt
Height:	4", 10.1 cm
Colour:	Yellow coat and hat, blue trousers, black boots
Issued:	1994 to the present (© 1994)

Back Stamp	*U.S. $*	*Price* *Can. $*	*U.K. £*	*Aust. $*
BK-6	40.00	55.00	14.95	65.00

DB148
BATHTIME BUNNYKINS™

Designer:	Graham Tongue
Modeller:	Warren Platt
Height:	4", 10.1 cm
Colour:	White bathrobe with grey trim, yellow towel and duck
Issued:	1994 to the present (©1994)

Back Stamp	*U.S. $*	*Price* *Can. $*	*U.K. £*	*Aust. $*
BK-6	40.00	55.00	14.95	65.00

DB149
EASTER GREETINGS BUNNYKINS™

Designer:	Graham Tongue
Modeller:	Warren Platt
Height:	4 1/2", 11.4 cm
Colour:	Yellow, white and green
Issued:	1995 to the present (© 1994)

Back Stamp	*U.S. $*	*Price* *Can. $*	*U.K. £*	*Aust. $*
BK-6	50.00	—	—	—

DB150
WICKET KEEPER™

Designer:	Denise Andrews
Modeller:	Amanda Hughes-Lubeck
Height:	3 1/2", 8.9 cm
Colour:	White, beige and black
Issued:	1995

Note: Produced exclusively for U.K. International Ceramics Ltd. Special Edition of 1,000

Back Stamp	*U.S. $*	*Price Can. $*	*U.K. £*	*Aust. $*
BK-6 Special	100.00	100.00	38.00	250.00

DB151
PARTNERS IN COLLECTING™

Designer:	Walter Hayward
Modeller:	Albert Hallam
Height:	3", 7.6 cm
Colour:	Red, white and blue
Issued:	1995 - 1995
Varieties:	Also called Storytime Bunnykins, DB9, DB59

Note: Commissioned to celebrate the 15th anniversary of the RDICC and sold at the Club convention in Williamsburg

Back Stamp	*U.S. $*	*Price Can. $*	*U.K. £*	*Aust. $*
BK-6	45.00	49.95	—	—

DB152
BOY SKATER™

Designer:	Graham Tongue
Modeller:	Martyn Alcock
Height:	4 1/4", 10.8 cm
Colour:	Blue coat, brown pants, yellow hat, green boots and black skates
Issued:	1995 to the present

Back Stamp	*U.S. $*	*Price Can. $*	*U.K. £*	*Aust. $*
BK-6	40.00	60.00	16.95	—

DB153
GIRL SKATER BUNNYKINS™

Designer:	Graham Tongue
Modeller:	Martyn Alcock
Height:	3 1/2", 8.9 cm
Colour:	Green coat with white trim, pink dress, blue books, yellow skates
Issued:	1995 to the present

Back Stamp	*U.S. $*	*Price Can. $*	*U.K. £*	*Aust. $*
BK-6	40.00	60.00	16.95	—

Note: DB154 not issued

DB155
MOTHER'S DAY BUNNYKINS™

Designer:	Graham Tongue
Modeller:	Shane Ridge
Height:	3 1/2", 8.9 cm
Colour:	Brown and blue
Issued:	1995 to the present

Back Stamp	*U.S. $*	*Price Can. $*	*U.K. £*	*Aust. $*
BK-6	40.00	60.00	17.95	—

Note: DB156 not issued

DB157
GOODNIGHT BUNNYKINS™

Designer:	Graham Tongue
Modeller:	Shane Ridge
Height:	3 3/4", 9.5 cm
Colour:	Pink night gown, reddish brown teddy, blue and white base
Issued:	1995 to the present

Back Stamp	*U.S. $*	*Price Can. $*	*U.K. £*	*Aust. $*
BK-6	40.00	60.00	13.95	—

DB158
NEW BABY BUNNYKINS™

Designer:	Graham Tongue
Modeller:	Graham Tongue
Height:	3 3/4", 9.5 cm
Colour:	Blue dress with white trim, white cradle, pink pillow, yellow blanket
Issued:	1995 to the present

Back Stamp	*U.S. $*	*Price Can. $*	*U.K. £*	*Aust. $*
BK-6	40.00	60.00	15.95	—

DB160
OUT FOR A DUCK™

Designer:	Denise Andrews
Modeller:	Amanda Hughes-Lubeck
Height:	4", 10.1 cm
Colour:	White, beige and green
Issued:	1995

Note: Produced exclusively for U.K.International Ceramics Ltd. in a special edition of 1,250

Back Stamp	*U.S. $*	*Price Can. $*	*U.K. £*	*Aust. $*
BK-	75.00	95.00	38.00	—

DB161
JESTER BUNNYKINS™

Designer:	Denise Andrews
Modeller:	Shane Ridge
Height:	4 1/2", 11.9 cm
Colour:	Red, green and yellow
Issued:	1995

Note: Produced exclusively for U.K. International Ceramics Ltd. in a special edition of 1,500

Back Stamp	*U.S. $*	*Price Can. $*	*U.K. £*	*Aust. $*
BK-	42.00	125.00	42.00	175.00

Photograph not available at press time

DB6966A
CITY GENT TEAPOT™
First Version (City Gentleman Style)

Designer:	Unknown
Modeller:	Martyn Alcock
Height:	8", 20.3 cm
Colour:	Brown and black
Issued:	1994
Varieties:	DB6966B

BUNNYKINS TEAPOTS OF THE WORLD
Hand made and hand decorated
Royal Doulton®
BUNNYKINS®
LONDON CITY GENT
D 6966
© 1994 ROYAL DOULTON
SPECIAL EDITION OF 2,500

Note: Produced exclusively for John Sinclair, Sheffield in a limited edition of 2,500.

Back Stamp	*U.S. $*	*Price Can. $*	*U.K. £*	*Aust. $*
BK-D6966B	125.00	150.00	75.00	250.00

DB6966B
THE PRESIDENTIAL BUNNYKINS TEAPOT™
Second Versions (Uncle Sam Style)

Designer:	Unknown
Modeller:	Shane Ridge
Height:	8", 20.3 cm
Colour:	Red, white and blue
Issued:	1995
Varieties:	DB 6966A

BUNNYKINS TEAPOTS OF THE WORLD
Hand made and hand decorated
Royal Doulton®
BUNNYKINS®
U.S.A. PRESIDENT
D 6996
© 1995 ROYAL DOULTON
SPECIAL EDITION OF 2,500

Note: Produced exclusively for John Sinclair, Sheffield in a limited edition of 2,500.

Back Stamp	*U.S. $*	*Price Can. $*	*U.K. £*	*Aust. $*
BK-DB6966B	125.00	150.00	75.00	250.00

D6003
D6004
D6002
D6025
D6001
D6024

DAVID HAND'S ANIMALAND

1148
DINKUM PLATYPUS™

Designer: Arthur Gredington
Height: 4 1/4", 10.8 cm
Colour: Brown and beige platypus, green base
Issued: 1949-1955

Beswick Number	*U.S. $*	*Price Can. $*	*U.K. £*	*Aust. $*
1148	150.00	175.00	90.00	175.00

1150
ZIMMY LION™

Designer: Arthur Gredington
Height: 3 3/4", 9.5 cm
Colour: Brown lion with white face
Issued: 1949-1955

Beswick Number	*U.S. $*	*Price Can. $*	*U.K. £*	*Aust. $*
1150	400.00	475.00	250.00	225.00

1151
FELIA™

Designer: Arthur Gredington
Height: 4", 10.1 cm
Colour: Green cat
Issued: 1949-1955

Beswick Number	*U.S. $*	*Price Can. $*	*U.K. £*	*Aust. $*
1151	600.00	750.00	400.00	225.00

1152
GINGER NUTT™

Designer: Arthur Gredington
Height: 4", 10.1 cm
Colour: Brown and beige squirrel, green base
Issued: 1949-1955

Beswick Number	*U.S. $*	*Price Can. $*	*U.K. £*	*Aust. $*
1152	700.00	775.00	450.00	225.00

1153
HAZEL NUTT™

Designer: Arthur Gredington
Height: 3 3/4", 9.5 cm
Colour: Brown and beige squirrel, green base
Issued: 1949-1955

Beswick Number	*U.S. $*	*Price Can. $*	*U.K. £*	*Aust. $*
1153	700.00	775.00	450.00	225.00

1154
OSCAR OSTRICH™

Designer: Arthur Gredington
Height: 3 3/4", 9.5 cm
Colour: Beige and mauve, brown base
Issued: 1949-1955

Beswick Number	*U.S. $*	*Price Can. $*	*U.K. £*	*Aust. $*
1154	600.00	750.00	400.00	225.00

1155
DUSTY MOLE™

Designer: Arthur Gredington
Height: 3 1/2", 8.9 cm
Colour: Blue mole, white face
Issued: 1949-1955

Beswick Number	U.S. $	Price Can. $	U.K. £	Aust. $
1155	275.00	350.00	175.00	225.00

1156
LOOPY HARE™

Designer: Arthur Gredington
Height: 4 1/4", 10.8 cm
Colour: Brown and beige hare
Issued: 1949-1955

Beswick Number	U.S. $	Price Can. $	U.K. £	Aust. $
1156	400.00	475.00	250.00	225.00

ENGLISH COUNTRY FOLK

ECF1
HUNTSMAN FOX™

Designer:	Amanda Hughes-Lubeck
Height:	5 3/4", 14.6 cm
Colour:	Dark green jacket and cap, blue-grey trousers, green wellingtons
Issued:	1993 to the present

BESWICK
ECF 1
HUNTSMAN FOX

Beswick Number	*U.S. $*	*Price Can. $*	*U.K. £*	*Aust. $*
9150	57.00	85.00	22.50	95.00

ECF2
FISHERMAN OTTER™

Designer:	Warren Platt
Height:	5 3/4", 14.6 cm
Colour:	Yellow shirt and hat, dark green waistcoat, blue-grey trousers, green wellingtons
Issued:	1993 to the present

BESWICK
ECF 2
FISHERMAN OTTER

Beswick Number	*U.S. $*	*Price Can. $*	*U.K. £*	*Aust. $*
9152	57.00	85.00	22.50	95.00

ECF3
GARDENER RABBIT™

Designer:	Warren Platt
Height:	6", 15.0 cm
Colour:	White shirt, red pullover, blue trousers, grey hat, black wellingtons
Issued:	1993 to the present

BESWICK
ECF 3
GARDENER RABBIT

Beswick Number	*U.S. $*	*Price Can. $*	*U.K. £*	*Aust. $*
9155	57.00	85.00	22.50	95.00

ECF4
GENTLEMAN PIG™

Designer: Amanda Hughes-Lubeck
Height: 5 3/4", 14.6 cm
Colour: Brown suit
Issued: 1993 to the present

BESWICK ENGLAND
ECF 4
GENTLEMAN PIG

Beswick Number	*Price U.S. $*	*Can. $*	*U.K. £*	*Aust. $*
9149	57.00	85.00	22.50	95.00

ECF5
SHEPHERD SHEEPDOG™

Designer: Warren Platt
Height: 6 3/4", 17.2 cm
Colour: Yellow smock
Issued: 1993 to the present

BESWICK ENGLAND
ECF 5
SHEPHERD SHEEPDOG

Beswick Number	*Price U.S. $*	*Can. $*	*U.K. £*	*Aust. $*
9156	57.00	85.00	22.50	95.00

ECF6
HIKER BADGER™

Designer: Warren Platt
Height: 5 1/4", 13.3 cm
Colour: Yellow shirt, blue waistcoat, red cap and socks
Issued: 1993 to the present

BESWICK ENGLAND
ECF 6
HIKER BADGER

Beswick Number	*Price U.S. $*	*Can. $*	*U.K. £*	*Aust. $*
9157	57.00	85.00	22.50	95.00

ECF7
MRS. RABBIT BAKING™

Designer:	Martyn Alcock
Height:	5 1/2", 14.0 cm
Colour:	Mauve dress, white apron and cap
Issued:	1994 to the present

BESWICK ENGLAND
ECF 7
MRS RABBIT BAKING

Beswick Number	*U.S. $*	*Price Can. $*	*U.K. £*	*Aust. $*
Unknown	57.00	85.00	22.50	95.00

ECF8
THE LADY PIG™

Designer:	Amanda Hughes-Lubeck
Height:	5 1/2", 14.0 cm
Colour:	Green jacket, skirt and hat, brown umbrella
Issued:	1995 to the present

BESWICK ENGLAND
ECF 8
THE LADY PIG

Beswick Number	*U.S. $*	*Price Can. $*	*U.K. £*	*Aust. $*
Unknown	57.00	85.00	22.50	95.00

JOAN WELSH
ANGLUND

2272
ANGLUND BOY™

Designer:	Albert Hallam
Height:	4 1/2", 11.9 cm
Colour:	Green dungarees; brown hat
Issued:	1969-1971

Beswick Number	*U.S. $*	*Price Can. $*	*U.K. £*	*Aust. $*
2272	225.00	275.00	125.00	325.00

2293
ANGLUND GIRL WITH DOLL™

Designer:	Albert Hallam
Height:	4 1/2", 11.9 cm
Colour:	Green dress and bow; white apron
Issued:	1969-1971

Beswick Number	*U.S. $*	*Price Can. $*	*U.K. £*	*Aust. $*
2293	225.00	275.00	125.00	325.00

2317
ANGLUND GIRL WITH FLOWERS™

Designer:	Albert Hallam
Height:	4 3/4", 12.1 cm
Colour:	White dress; blue leggings; straw hat with blue ribbon
Issued:	1969-1971

Beswick Number	*U.S. $*	*Price Can. $*	*U.K. £*	*Aust. $*
2317	225.00	275.00	125.00	325.00

KITTY MCBRIDE

2526
A FAMILY MOUSE™

Designer: Graham Tongue
Height: 3 1/2", 8.9 cm
Colour: Brown, mauve and turquoise, light and dark green base
Issued: 1975-1983

Beswick Number	*U.S. $*	*Price Can. $*	*U.K. £*	*Aust. $*
2526	95.00	115.00	60.00	150.00

2527
A DOUBLE ACT™

Designer: Graham Tongue
Height: 3 1/2", 8.9 cm
Colour: Yellow, orange, brown, green and blue
Issued: 1975-1983

Beswick Number	*U.S. $*	*Price Can. $*	*U.K. £*	*Aust. $*
2527	100.00	125.00	70.00	150.00

2528
THE RACEGOER™

Designer: David Lyttleton
Height: 3 1/2", 8.9 cm
Colour: Brown and yellow, light and dark green base
Issued: 1975-1983

Beswick Number	*U.S. $*	*Price Can. $*	*U.K. £*	*Aust. $*
2528	60.00	75.00	40.00	150.00

2529
A GOOD READ™

Designer: David Lyttleton
Height: 2 1/2", 6.4 cm
Colour: Yellow, blue, brown and white
Issued: 1975-1983

Beswick Number	*U.S. $*	*Price Can. $*	*U.K. £*	*Aust. $*
2529	375.00	425.00	250.00	400.00

2530
LAZY BONES™

Designer: David Lyttleton
Height: 1 1/2", 3.8 cm
Colour: Blue, black and brown, green and white base
Issued: 1975-1983

Beswick Number	*U.S. $*	*Price Can. $*	*U.K. £*	*Aust. $*
2530	95.00	115.00	60.00	150.00

2531
A SNACK™

Designer: David Lyttleton
Height: 3 1/4", 8.3 cm
Colour: Brown, blue and yellow, green base
Issued: 1975-1983

Beswick Number	*U.S. $*	*Price Can. $*	*U.K. £*	*Aust. $*
2531	65.00	85.00	45.00	150.00

2532
STRAINED RELATIONS™

Designer:	David Lyttleton
Height:	3", 7.6 cm
Colour:	Brown, blue and green
Issued:	1975-1983

Beswick Number	*Price* *U.S. $*	*Can. $*	*U.K. £*	*Aust. $*
2532	80.00	100.00	55.00	120.00

2533
JUST GOOD FRIENDS™

Designer:	David Lyttleton
Height:	3", 7.6 cm
Colour:	Brown, yellow, blue, red and green
Issued:	1975-1983

Beswick Number	*Price* *U.S. $*	*Can. $*	*U.K. £*	*Aust. $*
2533	125.00	150.00	75.00	175.00

2565
THE RING™

Designer:	David Lyttleton
Height:	3 1/4", 8.3 cm
Colour:	Brown, white, purple and yellow
Issued:	1976-1983

Beswick Number	*Price* *U.S. $*	*Can. $*	*U.K. £*	*Aust. $*
2565	95.00	115.00	60.00	200.00

2566
GUILTY SWEETHEARTS™

Designer: David Lyttleton
Height: 2 1/4", 5.7 cm
Colour: Brown, yellow, green and white
Issued: 1976-1983

Beswick Number	*Price U.S. $*	*Can. $*	*U.K. £*	*Aust. $*
2566	95.00	110.00	60.00	175.00

2589
ALL I DO IS THINK OF YOU™

Designer: David Lyttleton
Height: 2 1/2", 6.4 cm
Colour: Brown, yellow and white
Issued: 1976 - 1983

Beswick Number	*Price U.S. $*	*Can. $*	*U.K. £*	*Aust. $*
2589	195.00	225.00	115.00	300.00

LITTLE LIKABLES

LL1
FAMILY GATHERING™
(Hen and Two Chicks)

Designer: Diane Griffiths
Height: 4 1/2", 11.9 cm
Colour: White hen and chicks, with yellow beaks, and gold comb on hen
Issued: 1985-1987

Beswick		*Price*		
Number	*U.S. $*	*Can. $*	*U.K. £*	*Aust. $*
LL1	50.00	70.00	35.00	75.00

LL2
WATCHING THE WORLD GO BY™
(Frog)

Designer: Robert Tabbenor
Height: 3 3/4", 9.5 cm
Colour: White frog, black and green eyes
Issued: 1985-1987

Beswick		*Price*		
Number	*U.S. $*	*Can. $*	*U.K. £*	*Aust. $*
LL2	90.00	110.00	60.00	100.00

LL3
HIDE AND SEEK™
(Pig and Two Piglets)

Designer: Robert Tabbenor
Height: 3 1/4", 8.3 cm
Colour: White pigs with pink noses, ears and tails
Issued: 1985-1987

Beswick		*Price*		
Number	*U.S. $*	*Can. $*	*U.K. £*	*Aust. $*
LL3	50.00	70.00	35.00	75.00

LL4
MY PONY™
(Pony)

Designer: Diane Griffiths
Height: 7 1/4", 18.4 cm
Colour: White pony with blue highlights in mane and tail
Issued: 1985-1987

Beswick Number	*U.S. $*	*Price Can. $*	*U.K. £*	*Aust. $*
LL4	70.00	90.00	50.00	100.00

LL5
ON TOP OF THE WORLD™
(Elephant)

Designer: Diane Griffiths
Height: 3 3/4", 9.5 cm
Colour: White elephant with black eyes and gold nails
Issued: 1985-1987

Beswick Number	*U.S. $*	*Price Can. $*	*U.K. £*	*Aust. $*
LL5	50.00	70.00	35.00	75.00

LL6
TREAT ME GENTLY™
(Fawn)

Designer: Diane Griffiths
Height: 4 1/2", 11.9 cm
Colour: White fawn with black and brown eyes, black nose and gold hoof
Issued: 1985-1987

Beswick Number	*U.S. $*	*Price Can. $*	*U.K. £*	*Aust. $*
LL6	50.00	70.00	35.00	75.00

LL7
OUT AT LAST™
(Duckling)

Designer: Robert Tabbenor
Height: 3 1/4", 8.3 cm
Colour: White duck with black and brown eyes and gold beak
Issued: 1985-1987

Beswick Number	*U.S. $*	*Price Can. $*	*U.K. £*	*Aust. $*
LL7	50.00	70.00	35.00	75.00

LL8
CATS CHORUS™

Designer: Robert Tabbenor
Height: 4 3/4", 12.1 cm
Colour: Two white cats with black and green eyes, black nose, pink ears and mouth
Issued: 1985-1987

Beswick Number	*U.S. $*	*Price Can. $*	*U.K. £*	*Aust. $*
LL8	50.00	70.00	35.00	75.00

LITTLE LOVABLES

LL1
HAPPY BIRTHDAY™

Designer: Amanda Hughes-Lubeck
Height: 4 1/2", 11.9 cm
Colour: White, pink and orange (gloss)
Issued: 1992-1994
Varieties: LL8; LL15; Also unnamed LL22

Model No.	U.S. $	Price Can. $	U.K. £	Aust. $
3328	25.00	30.00	15.00	50.00

LL2
I LOVE YOU™

Designer: Amanda Hughes-Lubeck
Height: 4 1/2", 11.9 cm
Colour: White, green and pink (gloss)
Issued: 1992-1994
Varieties: LL9, LL16; Also unnamed LL23

Model No.	U.S. $	Price Can. $	U.K. £	Aust. $
3320	25.00	30.00	15.00	50.00

LL3
GOD LOVES ME™

Designer: Amanda Hughes-Lubeck
Height: 3 3/4", 9.5 cm
Colour: White, green and turquoise (gloss)
Issued: 1992-1993
Varieties: LL10, LL17; Also called "Please" LL33, LL34;
Also unnamed LL24

Model No.	U.S. $	Price Can. $	U.K. £	Aust. $
3336	50.00	75.00	35.00	50.00

LL4
JUST FOR YOU™

Designer: Warren Platt
Height: 4 1/2", 11.9 cm
Colour: White, pink and blue (gloss)
Issued: 1992-1994
Varieties: LL11, LL18; Also unnamed LL25

Model No.	*U.S. $*	*Price Can. $*	*U.K. £*	*Aust. $*
3361	25.00	30.00	15.00	50.00

LL5
TO MOTHER™

Designer: Amanda Hughes-Lubeck
Height: 4 1/2", 11.9 cm
Colour: White, blue and purple (gloss)
Issued: 1992-1994
Varieties: LL12, LL19; Also called "To Daddy"; Also unnamed LL26

Model No.	*U.S. $*	*Price Can. $*	*U.K. £*	*Aust. $*
3331	25.00	30.00	15.00	50.00

LL6
CONGRATULATIONS™

Designer: Warren Platt
Height: 4 1/2", 11.9 cm
Colour: White, green and pink (gloss)
Issued: 1992-1994
Varieties: LL13, LL20; Also unnamed LL27

Model No.	*U.S. $*	*Price Can. $*	*U.K. £*	*Aust. $*
3340	25.00	30.00	15.00	50.00

LL7
PASSED™

Designer: Amanda Hughes-Lubeck
Height: 3", 7.6 cm
Colour: White, lilac and pink (gloss)
Issued: 1992-1994
Varieties: LL14, LL21; Also unnamed LL28

Model No.	*U.S. $*	*Price Can. $*	*U.K. £*	*Aust. $*
3334	25.00	30.00	15.00	50.00

LL8
HAPPY BIRTHDAY™

Designer: Amanda Hughes-Lubeck
Height: 4 1/2", 11.9 cm
Colour: White, yellow and green (gloss)
Issued: 1992-1994
Varieties: LL1, LL15; Also unnamed LL22

Model No.	*U.S. $*	*Price Can. $*	*U.K. £*	*Aust. $*
3328	25.00	30.00	15.00	50.00

LL9
I LOVE YOU™

Designer: Amanda Hughes-Lubeck
Height: 4 1/2", 11.9 cm
Colour: White, blue and orange (gloss)
Issued: 1992-1994
Varieties: LL2, LL16; Also unnamed LL23

Model No.	*U.S. $*	*Price Can. $*	*U.K. £*	*Aust. $*
3320	25.00	30.00	15.00	50.00

LL10
GOD LOVES ME™

Designer: Amanda Hughes-Lubeck
Height: 3 3/4", 9.5 cm
Colour: White, gold and blue (gloss)
Issued: 1992-1993
Varieties: LL3, LL17; Also called "Please", LL33, LL34; Also unnamed LL24

Model No.	*U.S. $*	*Price Can. $*	*U.K. £*	*Aust. $*
3336	50.00	75.00	35.00	70.00

LL11
JUST FOR YOU™

Designer: Warren Platt
Height: 4 1/2", 11.9 cm
Colour: White, yellow and pale green (gloss)
Issued: 1992-1994
Varieties: LL4, LL18; Also unnamed LL25

Model No.	*U.S. $*	*Price Can. $*	*U.K. £*	*Aust. $*
3361	25.00	30.00	15.00	50.00

LL12
TO MOTHER™

Designer: Amanda Hughes-Lubeck
Height: 4 1/2", 11.9 cm
Colour: White, yellow and pink (gloss)
Issued: 1992-1994
Varieties: LL5, LL19; Also called "To Daddy" LL29; Also unnamed LL26

Model No.	*U.S. $*	*Price Can. $*	*U.K. £*	*Aust. $*
3331	25.00	30.00	15.00	50.00

LL13
CONGRATULATIONS™

Designer: Warren Platt
Height: 4 1/2", 11.9 cm
Colour: White, pale blue and yellow (gloss)
Issued: 1992-1994
Varieties: LL6, LL20; Also unnamed LL27

Model No.	*Price U.S. $*	*Can. $*	*U.K. £*	*Aust. $*
3340	25.00	30.00	15.00	50.00

LL14
PASSED™

Designer: Amanda Hughes-Lubeck
Height: 3", 7.6 cm
Colour: White, light blue and orange (gloss)
Issued: 1992-1994
Varieties: LL7, LL21; Also unnamed LL28

Model No.	*Price U.S. $*	*Can. $*	*U.K. £*	*Aust. $*
3334	25.00	30.00	15.00	50.00

LL15
HAPPY BIRTHDAY™

Designer: Amanda Hughes-Lubeck
Height: 4 1/2", 11.9cm
Colour: White, salmon and green (matt)
Issued: 1992-1993
Varieties: LL8, LL15; Also unnamed LL22

Model No.	*Price U.S. $*	*Can. $*	*U.K. £*	*Aust. $*
3407	90.00	120.00	60.00	50.00

LL16
I LOVE YOU™

Designer: Amanda Hughes-Lubeck
Height: 4 1/2", 11.9 cm
Colour: White, green and yellow (matt)
Issued: 1992-1993
Varieties: LL2, LL9; Also unnamed LL23

Model No.	*Price U.S. $*	*Can. $*	*U.K. £*	*Aust. $*
3406	90.00	120.00	60.00	50.00

LL17
GOD LOVES ME™

Designer: Amanda Hughes-Lubeck
Height: 3 3/4", 9.5 cm
Colour: White, purple and yellow (matt)
Issued: 1992-1993
Varieties: LL3, LL10; Also called "Please", LL33, LL34; Also unnamed LL24

Model No.	*Price U.S. $*	*Can. $*	*U.K. £*	*Aust.*
3410	120.00	150.00	80.00	70.00

LL18
JUST FOR YOU™

Designer: Warren Platt
Height: 4 1/2", 11.9 cm
Colour: White, yellow and dark blue (matt)
Issued: 1992-1993
Varieties: LL4, LL11; Also unnamed LL25

Model No.	*Price U.S. $*	*Can. $*	*U.K. £*	*Aust. $*
3412	90.00	120.00	60.00	50.00

LL19
TO MOTHER™

Designer: Amanda Hughes-Lubeck
Height: 4 1/2", 11.9 cm
Colour: White, green and orange (matt)
Issued: 1992-1993
Varieties: LL5, LL12; Also called "To Daddy" LL29; Also unnamed LL26

Model		*Price*		
No.	*U.S. $*	*Can. $*	*U.K. £*	*Aust. $*
3408	90.00	120.00	60.00	50.00

LL20
CONGRATULATIONS™

Designer: Warren Platt
Height: 4 1/2", 11.9 cm
Colour: White, blue and red (matt)
Issued: 1992-1993
Varieties: LL6, LL13; Also unnamed LL27

Model		*Price*		
No.	*U.S. $*	*Can. $*	*U.K. £*	*Aust. $*
3411	90.00	120.00	60.00	50.00

LL21
PASSED™

Designer: Amanda Hughes-Lubeck
Height: 3", 7.6 cm
Colour: White, blue and orange (matt)
Issued: 1992-1993
Varieties: LL7, LL14; Also unnamed LL28

Model		*Price*		
No.	*U.S. $*	*Can. $*	*U.K. £*	*Aust. $*
3409	90.00	120.00	60.00	50.00

LL22
(No Name)

Designer:	Unknown
Height:	4 1/2", 11.9 cm
Colour:	White, pink and orange (gloss)
Issued:	1993-1993
Varieties:	Also called "Happy Birthday", LL1, LL8, LL15

Model		*Price*		
No.	***U.S. $***	***Can. $***	***U.K. £***	***Aust. $***
3329	30.00	45.00	20.00	50.00

LL23
(No Name)

Designer:	Amanda Hughes-Lubeck
Height:	4 1/2", 11.9 cm
Colour:	White, green and pink (gloss)
Issued:	1993-1993
Varieties:	Also called "I Love You", LL2, LL9, LL16

Model		*Price*		
No.	***U.S. $***	***Can. $***	***U.K. £***	***Aust. $***
3320	30.00	45.00	20.00	50.00

LL24
(No Name)

Designer:	Amanda Hughes-Lubeck
Height:	3 3/4", 9.5 cm
Colour:	White, green and turquoise (gloss)
Issued:	1993-1993
Varieties:	Also called "God Loves Me" LL3, LL10, LL17; Also called "Please" LL33, LL34

Model		*Price*		
No.	***U.S. $***	***Can. $***	***U.K. £***	***Aust. $***
3336	30.00	45.00	20.00	50.00

LL25
(No Name)

Designer: Warren Platt
Height: 4 1/2", 11.9 cm
Colour: White, pink and blue (gloss)
Issued: 1993-1993
Varieties: Also called "Just For You" LL4, LL11, LL18

Model		*Price*		
No.	*U.S. $*	*Can. $*	*U.K. £*	*Aust. $*
3361	30.00	45.00	20.00	50.00

LL26
(No Name)

Designer: Amanda Hughes-Lubeck
Height: 4 1/4", 10.8 cm
Colour: White, blue and purple (gloss)
Issued: 1993-1993
Varieties: Also called "To Mother" LL5, LL12, LL19;
Also called "To Daddy" LL29

Model		*Price*		
No.	*U.S. $*	*Can. $*	*U.K. £*	*Aust. $*
3331	30.00	45.00	20.00	50.00

LL27
(No Name)

Designer: Warren Platt
Height: 4 1/2", 11.9 cm
Colour: White, green and pink (gloss)
Issued: 1993-1993
Varieties: Also called "Congratulations" LL6, LL13, LL20

Model		*Price*		
No.	*U.S. $*	*Can. $*	*U.K. £*	*Aust. $*
3340	30.00	45.00	20.00	50.00

LL28
(No Name)

Designer: Amanda Hughes-Lubeck
Height: 3", 7.6 cm
Colour: White, lilac and pink
Issued: 1993-1993
Varieties: Also called "Passed" LL7, LL14, LL21

Model No.	*U.S. $*	*Price Can. $*	*U.K. £*	*Aust. $*
3334	30.00	45.00	20.00	50.00

LL29
TO DADDY™

Designer: Amanda Hughes-Lubeck
Height: 4 1/2", 11.9 cm
Colour: White, light blue and green (gloss)
Issued: 1994-1994
Varieties: Also called "To Mother" LL5, LL12, LL19;
Also unnamed LL26

Model No.	*U.S. $*	*Price Can. $*	*U.K. £*	*Aust. $*
3331	25.00	30.00	15.00	50.00

LL30
MERRY CHRISTMAS™

Designer: Amanda Hughes-Lubeck
Height: 4", 10.1 cm
Colour: White, red and green (gloss)
Issued: 1993-1994

Model No.	*U.S. $*	*Price Can. $*	*U.K. £*	*Aust. $*
3389	25.00	30.00	15.00	50.00

LL31
GOOD LUCK™

Designer:	Amanda Hughes-Lubeck
Height:	4 1/4", 10.8 cm
Colour:	White, pink and green (gloss)
Issued:	1993-1994

Model No.	U.S. $	Price Can. $	U.K. £	Aust. $
3388	25.00	30.00	15.00	50.00

LL32
GET WELL SOON™

Designer:	Amanda Hughes-Lubeck
Height:	4 1/4", 10.8 cm
Colour:	White, green and purple (gloss)
Issued:	1994-1994

Model No.	U.S. $	Price Can. $	U.K. £	Aust. $
3390	25.00	30.00	15.00	50.00

LL33
PLEASE™

Designer:	Amanda Hughes-Lubeck
Height:	3 3/4", 9.5 cm
Colour:	White, green and blue (gloss)
Issued:	1993-1994
Varieties:	LL34; Also called "God Loves Me"; LL3, LL10, LL17; Also unnamed LL24

Model No.	U.S. $	Price Can. $	U.K. £	Aust. $
3336	25.00	30.00	15.00	50.00

LL34
PLEASE™

Designer:	Amanda Hughes-Lubeck
Height:	3 3/4", 9.5 cm
Colour:	White, gold and light blue (gloss)
Issued:	1993-1994
Varieties:	LL33; Also called "God Loves Me"; LL3, LL10, LL17; Also unnamed LL24

Model	*Price*			
No.	*U.S. $*	*Can. $*	*U.K. £*	*Aust. $*
3336	25.00	30.00	15.00	50.00

Photograph not available at press time

LL35
I LOVE BESWICK™

Designer:	Amanda Hughes-Lubeck
Height:	4 1/2", 11.9 cm
Colour:	White, green and yellow (Gloss)
Issued:	1995-1995

Note: This piece was specially commissioned for the Beswick Collectors Circle.

Model	*Price*			
No.	*U.S. $*	*Can. $*	*U.K. £*	*Aust. $*
3320	40.00	60.00	25.00	50.00

THE PIG PROMENADE

PP1
JOHN THE CONDUCTOR™
(Vietnamese Pot Bellied Pig)

Designer:	Martyn Alcock
Height:	4 3/4", 12.1 cm
Colour:	Black jacket, black bow tie
Issued:	1993 to the present

Beswick Ware
JOHN
PP 1

Back Stamp	*U.S. $*	*Price Can. $*	*U.K. £*	*Aust. $*
PP1	60.00	85.00	22.50	95.00

PP2
MATTHEW THE TRUMPET PLAYER™
(Large White Pig)

Designer:	Amanda Hughes-Lubeck
Height:	5", 12.7 cm
Colour:	Light red waistcoat, black bow tie
Issued:	1993 to the present

Beswick Ware
MATTHEW
PP 2

Back Stamp	*U.S. $*	*Price Can. $*	*U.K. £*	*Aust. $*
PP2	60.00	85.00	22.50	95.00

PP3
DAVID THE FLUTE PLAYER™
(Tamworth Pig)

Designer:	Amanda Hughes-Lubeck
Height:	5 1/4", 13.3 cm
Colour:	Dark green waistcoat, black bow tie
Issued:	1993 to the present

Beswick Ware
DAVID
PP 3

Back Stamp	*U.S. $*	*Price Can. $*	*U.K. £*	*Aust. $*
PP3	60.00	85.00	22.50	95.00

PP4
ANDREW THE CYMBAL PLAYER™
(Gloucester Old Spotted Pig)

Designer: Martyn Alcock
Height: 4 3/4", 12.1 cm
Colour: Purple waistcoat, yellow cymbals, black bow tie
Issued: 1993 to the present

Beswick Ware
ANDREW
PP 4

Back Stamp	*U.S. $*	*Price Can. $*	*U.K. £*	*Aust. $*
PP4	60.00	85.00	22.50	95.00

PP5
DANIEL THE VIOLINIST™
(Saddleback Pig)

Designer: Amanda J. Hughes-Lubeck
Height: 5 1/4", 13.3 cm
Colour: Pale blue waistcoat, brown violin
Issued: 1993 to the present

Beswick Ware
DANIEL
PP 5

Back Stamp	*U.S. $*	*Price Can. $*	*U.K. £*	*Aust. $*
PP5	60.00	85.00	22.50	95.00

PP6
MICHAEL THE BASS DRUM PLAYER™
(Large Black Pig)

Designer: Martyn Alcock
Height: 4 3/4", 12.1 cm
Colour: Yellow waistcoat, red and white drum
Issued: 1993 to the present

Beswick Ware
MICHAEL
PP 6

Back Stamp	*U.S. $*	*Price Can. $*	*U.K. £*	*Aust. $*
PP6	60.00	85.00	22.50	95.00

PP7
JAMES THE TRIANGLE PLAYER™
(Tamworth Piglet)

Designer: Warren Platt
Height: 4", 10.1 cm
Colour: Purple waistcoat; black bow tie
Issued: 1995 to the present

Back Stamp	*U.S. $*	*Can. $*	*Price U.K. £*	*Aust. $*
PP7	60.00	85.00	19.95	95.00

RUPERT BEAR

Photograph not available at press time

2694
RUPERT BEAR™

Designer:	Harry Sales
Height:	4 1/4", 10.8 cm
Colour:	Red sweater, yellow check trousers and scarf
Issued:	1980-1986

Beswick Number	*U.S. $*	*Price Can. $*	*U.K. £*	*Aust. $*
2694	400.00	475.00	250.00	400.00

2710
ALGY PUG™

Designer:	Harry Sales
Height:	4", 10.1 cm
Colour:	Grey jacket, yellow waistcoat, brown trousers
Issued:	1981-1986

Beswick Number	*U.S. $*	*Price Can. $*	*U.K. £*	*Aust. $*
2710	165.00	195.00	100.00	150.00

2711
PONG PING™

Designer:	Harry Sales
Height:	4 1/4", 10.8
Colour:	Dark green jacket; gold trousers
Issued:	1981-1986

Beswick Number	*U.S. $*	*Price Can. $*	*U.K. £*	*Aust. $*
2711	165.00	195.00	100.00	150.00

2720
BILL BADGER™

Designer:	Harry Sales
Height:	2 3/4", 7.0 cm
Colour:	Dark grey jacket, light grey trousers and red bow tie
Issued:	1981-1986

Beswick Number	*U.S. $*	*Price Can. $*	*U.K. £*	*Aust. $*
2720	165.00	195.00	100.00	150.00

2779
RUPERT BEAR SNOWBALLING™

Designer:	Harry Sales
Height:	4 1/4", 10.8 cm
Colour:	Red coat, yellow with brown striped trousers and scarf
Issued:	1982-1986

Beswick Number	*U.S. $*	*Price Can. $*	*U.K. £*	*Aust. $*
2779	400.00	475.00	250.00	450.00

THE SNOWMAN
GIFT COLLECTION

DS 1
JAMES™

Designer: Harry Sales
Modeller: David Lyttleton
Height: 3 3/4", 9.5 cm
Colour: Blue and white striped pyjamas brown dressing gown
Issued: 1985 - 1993 © 1985 R.D. (U.K.) © S.ENT. 1985

Royal Doulton®
THE SNOWMAN™
GIFT COLLECTION
JAMES
DS 1
© 1985 ROYAL DOULTON (UK)
© S.ENT 1985

Back Stamp	Price U.S. $	Can. $	U.K. £	Aust. $
DS-1	100.00	125.00	30.00	100.00

DS 2
THE SNOWMAN™

Designer: Harry Sales
Modeller: David Lyttleton
Height: 5", 12.7 cm
Colour: Green hat and scarf
Issued: 1985 - 1994
©1985 R.D. (U.K.) © S.ENT. 1985

Royal Doulton®
THE SNOWMAN™
GIFT COLLECTION
THE SNOWMAN
DS 2
© 1985 ROYAL DOULTON (UK)
© S.ENT 1985

Back Stamp	Price U.S. $	Can. $	U.K. £	Aust. $
DS-1	85.00	110.00	35.00	75.00

DS 3
STYLISH SNOWMAN™

Designer: Harry Sales
Modeller: David Lyttleton
Height: 5", 12.7 cm
Colour: Blue trousers, lilac braces, grey hat, yellow tie with red stripes.
Issued: 1985 - 1993
© 1985 R.D. (U.K.) © S.ENT.1985

Royal Doulton®
THE SNOWMAN™
GIFT COLLECTION
STYLISH SNOWMAN
DS 3
© 1985 ROYAL DOULTON (UK)
© S.ENT 1985

Back Stamp	Price U.S. $	Can. $	U.K. £	Aust. $
DS-1	85.00	110.00	40.00	100.00

DS 4
THANK YOU SNOWMAN™

Designer: Harry Sales
Modeller: David Lyttleton
Height: 5", 12.7 cm
Colour: Snowman has green hat and scarf; James wears a brown dressing gown
Issued: 1985 - 1994
© 1985 R.D. (U.K.) © S.ENT.1985

Royal Doulton®
THE SNOWMAN™
GIFT COLLECTION
THANK YOU SNOWMAN
DS 4
© 1985 ROYAL DOULTON (UK)
© S.ENT 1985

Back Stamp	U.S. $	Price Can. $	U.K. £	Aust. $
DS-1	85.00	125.00	30.00	75.00

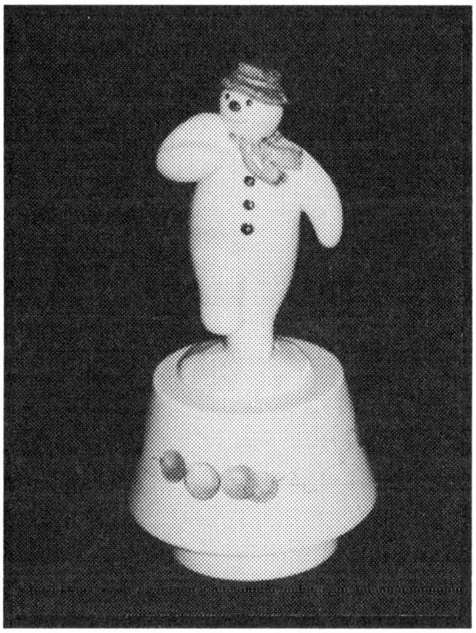

DS 5
SNOWMAN MAGIC - MUSIC BOX™

Designer: Harry Sales
Modeller: David Lyttleton
Height: 8", 20.3 cm
Colour: Cream music box with blue, green and pink balloon design
Issued: 1985 - 1994
© 1985 R.D. (U.K.) © S.ENT.1985
Tune: "Walking in the Air"

Back Stamp	U.S. $	Price Can. $	U.K. £	Aust. $
DS-1	125.00	150.00	60.00	100.00

DS 6
COWBOY SNOWMAN™

Designer: Harry Sales
Modeller: David Lyttleton
Height: 5", 12.7 cm
Colour: Brown hat and holster belt
Issued: 1986 - 1992
© 1985 R.D. (U.K.) © S.ENT.1985

Royal Doulton®
THE SNOWMAN™
GIFT COLLECTION
COWBOY SNOWMAN
DS 6
© 1985 ROYAL DOULTON (UK)
© S.ENT 1985

Back Stamp	U.S. $	Price Can. $	U.K. £	Aust. $
DS-1	275.00	225.00	70.00	125.00

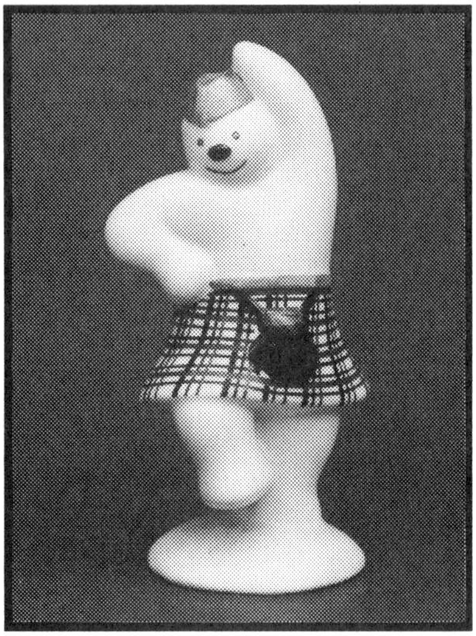

DS 7
HIGHLAND SNOWMAN™

Designer:	Harry Sales
Modeller:	David Lyttleton
Height:	5 1/4", 13.3 cm
Colour:	Red, blue and white kilt
Issued:	1987 - 1993
	© 1985 R.D. (U.K.) © S.ENT. 1985

Back Sstamp	*U.S. $*	*Price Can. $*	*U.K. £*	*Aust. $*
DS-1	85.00	110.00	50.00	100.00

DS 8
LADY SNOWMAN™

Designer:	Harry Sales
Modeller:	David Lyttleton
Height:	5", 12.7 cm
Colour:	Pink apron, blue hat
Issued:	1987 - 1992
	© 1985 R.D. (U.K.) © S.ENT. 1985

Back Stamp	*U.S. $*	*Price Can. $*	*U.K. £*	*Aust. $*
DS-1	100.00	135.00	70.00	150.00

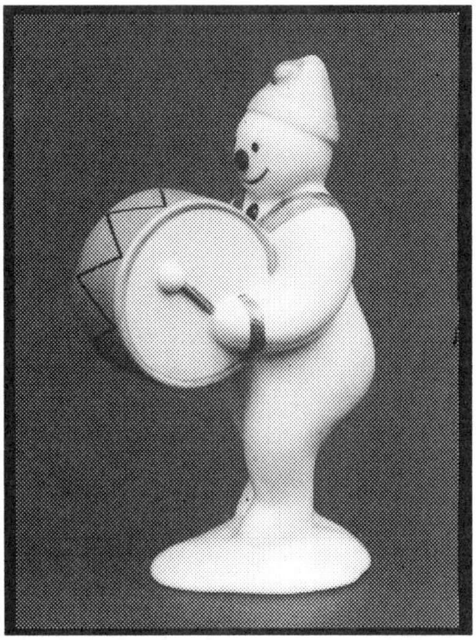

DS 9
BASS DRUMMER SNOWMAN™

Designer:	Graham Tongue
Modeller:	Warren Platt
Height:	5 1/2", 13.3 cm
Colour:	Pink and yellow drum, brown straps; pale blue hat
Issued:	1987 - 1993
	© 1987 R.D. © S.ENT. 1987

Back Stamp	*U.S. $*	*Price Can. $*	*U.K. £*	*Aust. $*
DS-1	85.00	110.00	45.00	125.00

DS 10
FLAUTIST SNOWMAN™

Designer: Graham Tongue
Modeller: Warren Platt
Height: 5 1/2", 14.0 cm
Colour: Yellow and red cap, brown tie
Issued: 1987 - 1993
© 1987 R.D. © S. ENT 1987

Royal Doulton®
THE SNOWMAN™
GIFT COLLECTION
FLAUTIST SNOWMAN
DS 10
© 1987 ROYAL DOULTON
© S. ENT 1987

Back Stamp	Price U.S. $	Can. $	U.K. £	Aust. $
DS-1	85.00	110.00	45.00	125.00

DS 11
VIOLINIST SNOWMAN™

Designer: Graham Tongue
Modeller: Warren Platt
Height: 5 1/4", 13.3 cm
Colour: Green waistcoat with yellow collar, brown cap and violin, blue bow tie
Issued: 1987 - 1994
© 1988 R.D. © S. ENT 1988

Royal Doulton®
THE SNOWMAN™
GIFT COLLECTION
VIOLINIST SNOWMAN
DS 11
© 1987 ROYAL DOULTON
© S. ENT 1987

Back Stamp	Price U.S. $	Can. $	U.K. £	Aust. $
DS-1	85.00	110.00	40.00	125.00

DS 12
PIANIST SNOWMAN™

Designer: Graham Tongue
Modeller: Warren Platt
Height: 5", 12.7 cm
Colour: Blue crown, orange tie
Issued: 1987 - 1994
© 1987 R.D. © S.ENT. 1987

Royal Doulton®
THE SNOWMAN™
GIFT COLLECTION
PIANIST SNOWMAN
DS 12
© 1987 ROYAL DOULTON
© S. ENT 1987

Back Stamp	Price U.S. $	Can. $	U.K. £	Aust. $
DS-1	65.00	75.00	30.00	100.00

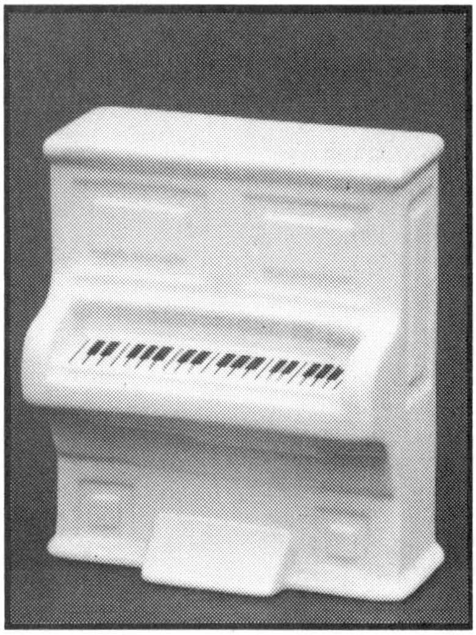

DS 13
SNOWMAN'S PIANO™

Designer: Graham Tongue
Modeller: Warren Platt
Height: 5", 13.3 cm
Colour: White
Issued: 1987 - 1994
© 1987 R.D. © S.ENT. 1987

Back Sstamp	*U.S. $*	*Price Can. $*	*U.K. £*	*Aust. $*
DS-1	65.00	80.00	20.00	100.00

DS 14
CYMBAL PLAYER SNOWMAN™

Designer: Graham Tongue
Modeller: Warren Platt
Height: 5 1/4", 13.3 cm
Colour: Brown waistcoat, green cap and bow tie, yellow cymbals
Issued: 1988 - 1993
© 1988 R.D. © S. ENT 1988

Back Sstamp	*U.S. $*	*Price Can. $*	*U.K. £*	*Aust. $*
DS-1	85.00	110.00	35.00	125.00

DS 15
DRUMMER SNOWMAN™

Designer: Graham Tongue
Modeller: Warren Platt
Height: 5 3/4", 14.6 cm
Colour: Red and black hat, purple bow tie, pink and yellow drum
Issued: 1988 - 1994
© 1988 R.D. © S. ENT 1988

Back Stamp	*U.S. $*	*Price Can. $*	*U.K. £*	*Aust. $*
DS-1	85.00	110.00	30.00	120.00

DS 16
TRUMPETER SNOWMAN™

Designer: Graham Tongue
Modeller: Warren Platt
Height: 5", 12.7 cm
Colour: Pink hat, yellow trumpet
Issued: 1988-1993
© 1988 R.D. © S. ENT 1988

Back Stamp	*U.S. $*	*Price Can. $*	*U.K. £*	*Aust. $*
DS-1	85.00	110.00	40.00	125.00

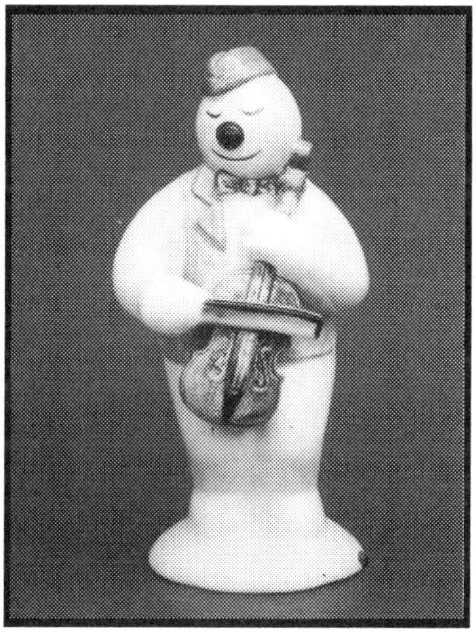

DS 17
CELLIST SNOWMAN™

Designer: Graham Tongue
Modeller: Warren Platt
Height: 5 1/4", 13.3 cm
Colour: Green waistcoat with yellow collar, brown coat and cello, blue bow tie
Issued: 1988 - 1993
© 1985 R.D. © S.ENT. 1985

Back Stamp	*U.S. $*	*Price Can. $*	*U.K. £*	*Aust. $*
DS-1	85.00	110.00	35.00	125.00

DS 18
SNOWMAN MUSICAL BOX™

Designer: Unknown
Height: 8", 22.5 cm
Colour: Unknown
Issued: 1988 - 1990
Tune: Blue Bells of Scotland

Back Sstamp	*U.S. $*	*Price Can. $*	*U.K. £*	*Aust. $*
DS-1	125.00	150.00	60.00	125.00

Photograph not available at press time

DS 19
SNOWMAN MONEY BOX™

Designer: Graham Tongue
Modeller: Warren Platt
Height: 8 1/2", 21.6 cm
Colour: Green hat and scarf with grey band
Issued: 1990 - 1994
© 1990 R.D. © S. ENT 1990

Back Stamp	*U.S. $*	*Price Can. $*	*U.K. £*	*Aust. $*
DS-1	125.00	140.00	40.00	100.00

DS 20
THE SNOWMAN TOBOGGANING™

Designer: Graham Tongue
Modeller: Warren Platt
Height: 5", 12.7 cm
Colour: Green hat and scarf, rose-pink toboggan
Issued: 1990 - 1994
© 1990 R.D. © S. ENT 1990

Back Stamp	*U.S. $*	*Price Can. $*	*U.K. £*	*Aust. $*
DS-1	150.00	175.00	50.00	100.00

DS 21
THE SNOWMAN SKIING™

Designer: Graham Tongue
Modeller: Warren Platt
Height: 5", 12.7 cm
Colour: Green hat and scarf, yellow and black goggles
Issued: 1990 - 1992
© 1990 R.D. © S.ENT. 1990

Back Stamp	*U.S. $*	*Price Can. $*	*U.K. £*	*Aust. $*
DS-1	250.00	300.00	375.00	125.00

DS 22
THE SNOWBALLING SNOWMAN™

Designer:	Graham Tongue
Modeller:	Warren Platt
Height:	5", 12.7 cm
Colour:	Green had and scarf, brown tree stump
Issued:	1990- 1994

Back Stamp	*U.S. $*	*Price* *Can. $*	*U.K. £*	*Aust. $*
DS1	100.00	125.00	50.00	100.00

DS 23
BUILDING THE SNOWMAN™

Designer:	Graham Tongue
Modeller:	Warren Platt
Height:	4", 10.1 cm
Colour:	Green hat and scarf
Issued:	1990 - 1994
	© 1990 R.D. © S.ENT 1990

Back Stamp	*U.S. $*	*Price* *Can. $*	*U.K. £*	*Aust.*
DS1	100.00	125.00	50.00	100.00

D6972
SNOWMAN MINIATURE CHARACTER JUG™

Designer:	Graham Tongue
Modeller:	Martyn Alcock
Height:	2 3/4", 7.0 cm
Colour:	White, black and green
Issued:	1994 to the present U.S.A. Exclusive

Back Stamp	*U.S. $*	*Can. $*	*Price* *U.K. £*	*Aust. $*
DS1	62.00	—	—	—

THELWELL

2704A
AN ANGEL ON HORSEBACK™

Designer:	Harry Sales
Modeller:	David Lyttleton
Height:	4 1/2", 11.9 cm
Colour:	Grey horse, rider wears brown jumper, yellow pants
Issued:	1981-1989
Varieties:	2704B

Beswick Number	*U.S. $*	*Price Can. $*	*U.K. £*	*Aust. $*
2704A	150.00	175.00	80.00	150.00

2704B
AN ANGEL ON HORSEBACK™

Designer:	Harry Sales
Modeller:	David Lyttleton
Height:	4 1/2", 11.9 cm
Colour:	Bay horse, rider wears red jumper, yellow pants
Issued:	1981-1989
Varieties:	2704A

Beswick Number	*U.S. $*	*Price Can. $*	*U.K. £*	*Aust. $*
2704B	125.00	150.00	70.00	135.00

2769A
KICK START™

Designer:	Harry Sales
Modeller:	David Lyttleton
Height:	3 1/2", 8.9 cm
Colour:	Grey horse, rider wears red jersey and yellow pants
Issued:	1982-1989
Varieties:	2769B

Beswick Number	*U.S. $*	*Price Can. $*	*U.K. £*	*Aust. $*
2769A	150.00	175.00	75.00	150.00

2769B
KICK START™

Designer:	Harry Sales
Modeller:	David Lyttleton
Height:	3 1/2", 8.9 cm
Colour:	Bay horse, rider wears red jersey and yellow pants
Issued:	1982-1989
Varieties:	2769B

Beswick Number	*Price U.S. $*	*Can. $*	*U.K. £*	*Aust. $*
2769B	125.00	150.00	60.00	135.00

2789A
PONY EXPRESS™

Designer:	Harry Sales
Modeller:	David Lyttleton
Height:	4 1/2", 11.9 cm
Colour:	Grey horse, rider wears green jersey and yellow trousers
Issued:	1982-1989
Varieties:	2789B

Beswick Number	*Price U.S. $*	*Can. $*	*U.K. £*	*Aust. $*
2789A	150.00	175.00	75.00	150.00

2789B
PONY EXPRESS™

Designer:	Harry Sales
Modeller:	David Lyttleton
Height:	4 1/2", 11.9 cm
Colour:	Bay horse, rider wears red jersey and yellow pants
Issued:	1982-1989
Varieties:	2789A

Beswick Number	*Price U.S. $*	*Can. $*	*U.K. £*	*Aust. $*
2789B	125.00	150.00	65.00	135.00

SS7 A
"I FORGIVE YOU"™

Designer: Harry Sales
Modeller: David Lyttleton
Height: 4", 10.1 cm
Colour: Grey horse, rider wears red jacket and yellow pants
Issued: 1985-1985
Series: Studio Sculptures
Varieties: SS7 B

Beswick Number	*Price U.S. $*	*Can. $*	*U.K. £*	*Aust. $*
SS7A	150.00	175.00	100.00	195.00

SS7 B
"I FORGIVE YOU"™

Designer: Harry Sales
Modeller: David Lyttleton
Height: 4", 10.1 cm
Colour: Bay horse, rider wears red jacket and yellow pants
Issued: 1985-1985
Series: Studio Sculptures
Varieties: SS7 A

Beswick Number	*Price U.S. $*	*Can. $*	*U.K. £*	*Aust. $*
SS7B	125.00	150.00	85.00	140.00

SS12 A
"EARLY BATH"™

Designer: Harry Sales
Modeller: David Lyttleton
Height: 4 3/4", 12.1 cm
Colour: Grey horse, rider wears red jacket and yellow pants
Issued: 1985-1985
Series: Studio Sculptures
Varieties: SS12 A

Beswick Number	*Price U.S. $*	*Can. $*	*U.K. £*	*Aust. $*
SS12A	200.00	225.00	125.00	200.00

SS12 B
"EARLY BATH"™

Designer:	
Height:	4 3/4", 12.1 cm
Colour:	Bay horse, rider wears red jacket and yellow pants
Issued:	1985-1985
Series:	Studio Sculptures
Varieties:	SS12 A

Beswick		*Price*		
Number	***U.S. $***	***Can. $***	***U.K. £***	***Aust. $***
SS12B	175.00	200.00	100.00	195.00

Photograph
not available
at press time

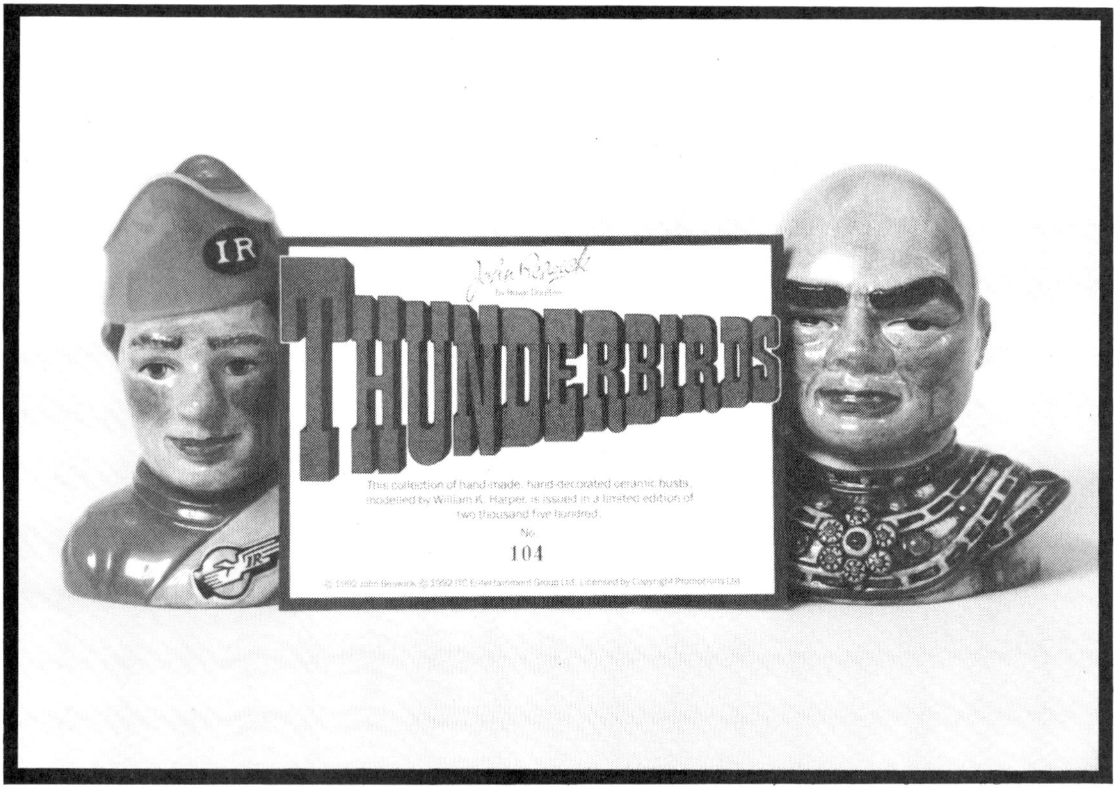
IR
THUNDERBIRDS
This collection of hand-made, hand-decorated ceramic busts, modelled by William K. Harper, is issued in a limited edition of two thousand five hundred.
No.
104
© 1992 John Beswick © 1992 ITC Entertainment Group Ltd. Licensed by Copyright Promotions Ltd

THUNDERBIRDS

3337
LADY PENELOPE™

Designer:	William K. Harper
Height:	4", 10.1 cm
Colour:	Pink hat and coat, blond hair
Issued:	1992 in a limited edition of 2,500

Beswick Number	*U.S. $*	*Price Can. $*	*U.K. £*	*Aust. $*
3337	£350.00 for complete set.			

3339
BRAINS™

Designer:	William K. Harper
Height:	4", 10.1 cm
Colour:	Black and blue uniform, blue glasses, black hair
Issued:	1992 in a limited edition of 2,500

Beswick Number	*U.S. $*	*Price Can. $*	*U.K. £*	*Aust. $*
3339	£350.00 for complete set.			

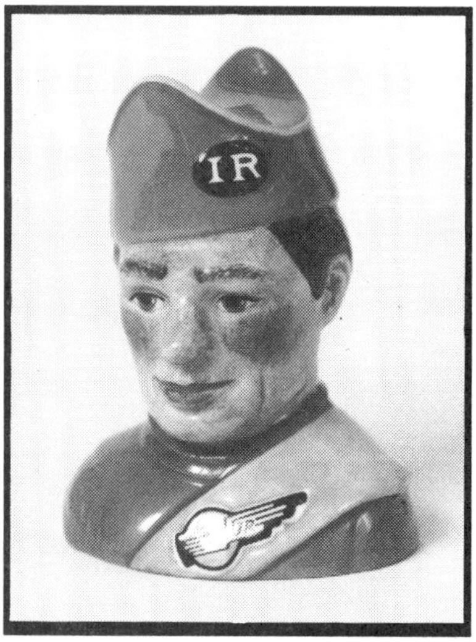

3344
SCOTT TRACY™

Designer:	William K. Harper
Height:	4", 10.1 cm
Colour:	Blue uniform, light blue band
Issued:	1992 in a limited edition of 2,500

Beswick Number	*U.S. $*	*Price Can. $*	*U.K. £*	*Aust. $*
3344	£350.00 for complete set.			

3345
VIRGIL TRACY™

Designer: William K. Harper
Height: 4", 10.1 cm
Colour: Blue uniform, yellow band
Issued: 1992 in a limited edition of 2,500

Beswick		*Price*		
Number	*U.S. $*	*Can. $*	*U.K. £*	*Aust. $*
3345	£350.00 for complete set.			

3346
PARKER™

Designer: William K. Harper
Height: 4", 10.1 cm
Colour: Blue-grey uniform
Issued: 1992 in a limited edition of 2,500

Beswick		*Price*		
Number	*U.S. $*	*Can. $*	*U.K. £*	*Aust. $*
3346	£350.00 for complete set.			

3348
THE HOOD™

Designer: William K. Harper
Height: 4", 10.1 cm
Colour: Browns
Issued: 1992 in a limited edition of 2,500

Beswick		*Price*		
Number	*U.S. $*	*Can. $*	*U.K. £*	*Aust. $*
3348	£350.00 for complete set.			

WALT DISNEY CHARACTERS

1278
MICKEY MOUSE™

Designer:	Jan Granoska
Height:	4", 10.1 cm
Colour:	Black, white and red
Issued:	1952-1965

Beswick		*Price*		
Number	*U.S. $*	*Can. $*	*U.K.£*	*Aust. $*
1278	450.00	575.00	350.00	350.00

1279
JIMINY CRICKET™

Designer:	Jan Granoska
Height:	4", 10.1 cm
Colour:	Black, white, beige and blue
Issued:	1952-1965

Beswick		*Price*		
Number	*U.S. $*	*Can. $*	*U.K. £*	*Aust. $*
1279	450.00	575.00	275.00	350.00

1280
PLUTO™

Designer:	Jan Granoska
Height:	3 1/2", 8.9 cm
Colour:	Brown dog with red collar
Issued:	1953-1965

Beswick		*Price*		
Number	*U.S. $*	*Can. $*	*U.K. £*	*Aust. $*
1280	450.00	550.00	325.00	350.00

1281
GOOFY™

Designer: Jan Granoska
Height: 4 1/4", 10.8 cm
Colour: Red jersey, blue trousers, black suspenders, white gloves, brown and black hat, brown boots
Issued: 1953-1965

Beswick Number	*U.S. $*	*Price Can. $*	*U.K. £*	*Aust. $*
1281	450.00	575.00	325.00	350.00

1282
PINOCCHIO™

Designer: Jan Granoska
Height: 4", 10.1 cm
Colour: White and yellow jacket, red trousers, blue bow tie and shoes, brown cap
Issued: 1953-1965

Beswick Number	*U.S. $*	*Price Can. $*	*U.K. £*	*Aust. $*
1282	450.00	550.00	275.00	350.00

1283
DONALD DUCK™

Designer: Jan Granoska
Height: 4", 10.1 cm
Colour: White duck, blue sailor's jacket, red bow, blue and black hat
Issued: 1953-1965

Beswick Number	*U.S. $*	*Price Can. $*	*U.K. £*	*Aust. $*
1282	450.00	575.00	300.00	350.00

Photograph not available at press time

1289
MINNIE MOUSE™

Designer: Jan Granoska
Height: 4", 10.1 cm
Colour: Unknown
Issued: 1953-1965

Beswick Number	*U.S. $*	*Price Can. $*	*U.K. £*	*Aust. $*
1289	450.00	575.00	350.00	350.00

1291
THUMPER™

Designer: Jan Granoska
Height: 3 3/4", 9.5 cm
Colour: Grey and white rabbit, yellow, red and pink flowers on brown base
Issued: 1953-1965

Beswick Number	*U.S. $*	*Price Can. $*	*U.K. £*	*Aust. $*
1291	850.00	750.00	300.00	350.00

1301
NANA™

Designer: Jan Granoska
Height: 3 1/4", 8.3 cm
Colour: Brown dog, white frilled cap with blue ribbon
Issued: 1953-1965

Beswick Number	*U.S. $*	*Price Can. $*	*U.K. £*	*Aust. $*
1301	450.00	550.00	300.00	350.00

1302
SMEE™

Designer: Jan Granoska
Height: 4 1/4", 10.8 cm
Colour: Blue and white shirt, blue pants, red cap, green bottle
Issued: 1953-1965

Beswick Number	*U.S. $*	*Price Can. $*	*U.K. £*	*Aust. $*
1302	450.00	600.00	175.00	350.00

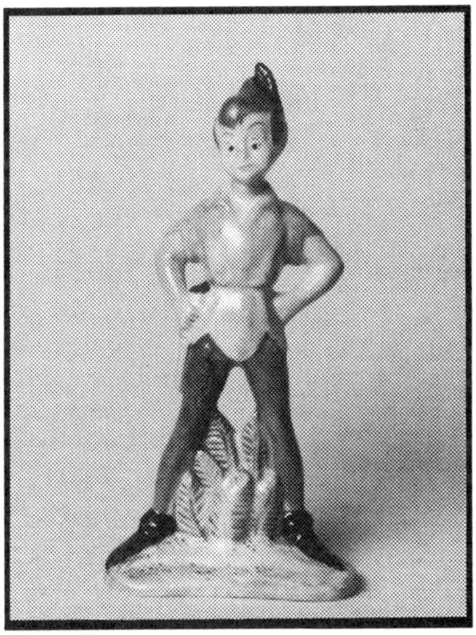

1307
PETER PAN™

Designer: Jan Granoska
Height: 5", 12.7 cm
Colour: Light green tunic, dark green pants, brown shoes, red and green cap
Issued: 1953-1965

Beswick Number	*U.S. $*	*Price Can. $*	*U.K. £*	*Aust. $*
1307	550.00	625.00	275.00	350.00

1312
TINKER BELL™

Designer: Jan Granoska
Height: 5", 12.7 cm
Colour: Light green dress, dark green wings and shoes
Issued: 1953-1965

Beswick Number	*U.S. $*	*Price Can. $*	*U.K. £*	*Aust. $*
1312		Rare		

1325
DOPEY™

Designer: Arthur Gredington
Height: 3 1/2", 8.9 cm
Colour: Green coat, maroon cap, grey shoes
Issued: 1954-1967

Dopey
COPYRIGHT
WALT DISNEY LTD
BESWICK
ENGLAND

Beswick Number	*U.S. $*	*Price Can. $*	*U.K. £*	*Aust. $*
1325	400.00	500.00	150.00	250.00

1326
HAPPY™

Designer: Arthur Gredington
Height: 3 1/2", 8.9 cm
Colour: Purple tunic, light blue trousers, light brown cap, brown shoes
Issued: 1954-1967

Happy
COPYRIGHT
WALT DISNEY LTD
BESWICK
ENGLAND

Beswick Number	*U.S. $*	*Price Can. $*	*U.K. £*	*Aust. $*
1326	400.00	500.00	150.00	250.00

1327
BASHFUL™

Designer: Arthur Gredington
Height: 3 1/2", 8.9 cm
Colour: Brown tunic, Purple trousers, grey cap, brown shoes
Issued: 1954-1967

Bashful
COPYRIGHT
WALT DISNEY LTD
BESWICK
ENGLAND

Beswick Number	*U.S. $*	*Price Can. $*	*U.K. £*	*Aust. $*
1327	400.00	500.00	150.00	250.00

1328
SNEEZY™

Designer: Arthur Gredington
Height: 3 1/2", 8.9 cm
Colour: Green tunic, purple trousers, brown cap and shoes
Issued: 1954-1967

Beswick Number	*U.S. $*	*Price Can. $*	*U.K. £*	*Aust. $*
1328	400.00	500.00	150.00	250.00

1329
DOC™

Designer: Arthur Gredington
Height: 3 1/2", 8.9 cm
Colour: Brown tunic, blue trousers, yellow cap, brown shoes
Issued: 1954-1967

Beswick Number	*U.S. $*	*Price Can. $*	*U.K. £*	*Aust. $*
1329	400.00	500.00	175.00	250.00

1330
GRUMPY™

Designer: Arthur Gredington
Height: 3 3/4", 9.5 cm
Colour: Purple tunic, red trousers, blue cap, brown shoes
Issued: 1954-1967

Beswick Number	*U.S. $*	*Price Can. $*	*U.K. £*	*Aust. $*
1330	400.00	500.00	150.00	250.00

1331
SLEEPY™

Designer:	Arthur Gredington
Height:	3 1/2", 8.9 cm
Colour:	Tan tunic, red trousers, green hat, grey shoes
Issued:	1954-1967

Beswick Number	*U.S. $*	*Price Can. $*	*U.K. £*	*Aust. $*
1331	400.00	500.00	150.00	250.00

1332 A
SNOW WHITE™
First Version (Hair in flounces)

Designer:	Arthur Gredington
Height:	5 1/2", 14.0 cm
Colour:	Yellow and purple dress, red cape, white collar
Issued:	1954-1955

Beswick Number	*U.S. $*	*Price Can. $*	*U.K. £*	*Aust. $*
1332A		Very Rare		

1332 B
SNOW WHITE™
Second Version (Hair flat to head)

Designer:	Arthur Gredington
Height:	5 1/2", 14.0 cm
Colour:	Yellow and purple dress, red cape, white collar
Issued:	1955-1967

Beswick Number	*U.S. $*	*Price Can. $*	*U.K. £*	*Aust. $*
1332B	750.00	875.00	375.00	500.00

2193
WINNIE THE POOH™

Designer: Albert Hallam
Height: 2 1/2", 6.4 cm
Colour: Golden brown and red
Issued: 1968-1990

Beswick Number	*U.S. $*	*Price Can. $*	*U.K. £*	*Aust. $*
GBS	100.00	175.00	100.00	190.00
BBS	80.00	125.00	85.00	135.00

2196
EEYORE™

Designer: Albert Hallam
Height: 2", 5.0 cm
Colour: Grey with black markings
Issued: 1968-1990

Beswick Number	*U.S. $*	*Price Can. $*	*U.K. £*	*Aust. $*
GBS 2	100.00	125.00	75.00	140.00
BBS 3	75.00	100.00	60.00	110.00

2214
PIGLET™

Designer: Albert Hallam
Height: 2 3/4", 7.0 cm
Colour: Pink and red
Issued: 1968-1990

Beswick Number	*U.S. $*	*Price Can. $*	*U.K. £*	*Aust. $*
GBS 2	125.00	150.00	80.00	165.00
BBS 3	100.00	125.00	65.00	140.00

2215
RABBIT™

Designer: Albert Hallam
Height: 3 1/4", 8.3 cm
Colour: Brown and beige
Issued: 1968-1990

Beswick Number	*U.S. $*	*Price Can. $*	*U.K. £*	*Aust. $*
GBS 2	100.00	175.00	70.00	190.00
BBS 3	80.00	125.00	55.00	135.00

2216
OWL™

Designer: Albert Hallam
Height: 3", 7.6 cm
Colour: Brown, white and black
Issued: 1968-1990

Beswick Number	*U.S. $*	*Price Can. $*	*U.K. £*	*Aust. $*
GBS 2	95.00	120.00	65.00	130.00
BBS 3	75.00	95.00	50.00	110.00

2217
KANGA™

Designer: Albert Hallam
Height: 3 1/4", 8.3 cm
Colour: Dark and light brown
Issued: 1968-1990

Beswick Number	*U.S. $*	*Price Can. $*	*U.K. £*	*Aust. $*
GBS 2	100.00	125.00	65.00	135.00
BBS 3	85.00	100.00	50.00	115.00

2394
TIGGER™

Designer: Graham Tongue
Height: 3", 7.6 cm
Colour: Yellow with black stripes
Issued: 1971-1990

Beswick Number	*Price* *U.S. $*	*Can. $*	*U.K. £*	*Aust. $*
GBS 2	225.00	250.00	115.00	275.00
BBS 3	200.00	225.00	95.00	250.00

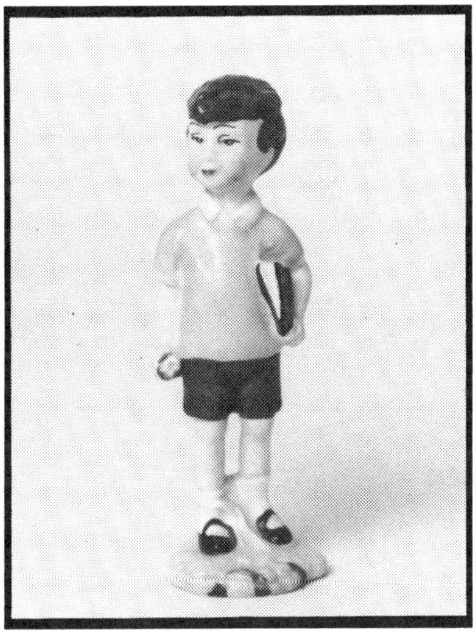

2395
CHRISTOPHER ROBIN™

Designer: Graham Tongue
Height: 4 3/4", 12.1 cm
Colour: Yellow, blue and white
Issued: 1971-1990

CHRISTOPHER ROBIN .
©
WALT DISNEY PROD
BESWICK ENGLAND

Beswick Number	*Price* *U.S. $*	*Can. $*	*U.K. £*	*Aust. $*
GBS 2	250.00	275.00	125.00	295.00
BBS 3	225.00	250.00	100.00	275.00

WIND IN THE WILLOWS

2939
MOLE™

Designer: Harry Sales
Modeller: David Lyttleton
Height: 3", 7.6 cm
Colour: Dark grey mole; brown dressing gown
Issued: 1987-1989

Beswick Number	*U.S. $*	*Price Can. $*	*U.K. £*	*Aust. $*
2939	65.00	85.00	40.00	75.00

2940
BADGER™

Designer: Harry Sales
Modeller: David Lyttleton
Height: 3", 7.6 cm
Colour: Black and white badger; salmon dressing gown
Issued: 1987-1989

Beswick Number	*U.S. $*	*Price Can. $*	*U.K. £*	*Aust. $*
2940	65.00	85.00	40.00	75.00

2941
RATTY™

Designer: Harry Sales
Modeller: David Lyttleton
Height: 3 1/2", 8.9 cm
Colour: Blue dungarees; white shirt
Issued: 1987-1989

Beswick Number	*U.S. $*	*Price Can. $*	*U.K. £*	*Aust. $*
2941	65.00	85.00	40.00	75.00

2942
TOAD™

Designer:	Harry Sales
Modeller:	David Lyttleton
Height:	3 1/2", 8.9 cm
Colour:	Green toad; yellow waistcoat and trousers; white shirt; red bow tie
Issued:	1987-1989

Beswick Number	*U.S. $*	*Price Can. $*	*U.K. £*	*Aust. $*
2942	65.00	85.00	40.00	75.00

3065
PORTLY™
(Otter)

Designer:	Harry Sales
Modeller:	Alan Maslankowski
Height:	2 3/4", 7.0 cm
Colour:	Brown otter; blue dungarees; green and yellow jumper; green shoes
Issued:	1988-1989

Beswick Number	*U.S. $*	*Price Can. $*	*U.K. £*	*Aust. $*
3065	160.00	190.00	100.00	125.00

3076
WEASEL GAMEKEEPER™

Designer:	Harry Sales
Modeller:	Alan Maslankowski
Height:	4", 10.1 cm
Colour:	Brown weasel; green jacket, trousers and cap; yellow waistcoat
Issued:	1988-1989

Beswick Number	*U.S. $*	*Price Can. $*	*U.K. £*	*Aust. $*
3076	175.00	200.00	115.00	125.00

MISCELLANEOUS

1026
CAT CONDUCTOR™

Designer:	Arthur Gredington
Height:	2", 5.0 cm
Colour:	Grey striped
Issued:	1945-1973
Series:	Cat Orchestra
Set:	1027, 1028, 1029

Beswick		*Price*		
Number	*U.S. $*	*Can. $*	*U.K.£*	*Aust. $*
1026	75.00	100.00	25.00	75.00

1027
CAT WITH CELLO™

Designer:	Arthur Gredington
Height:	2", 5.0 cm
Colour:	Grey striped
Issued:	1945-1973
Series:	Cat Orchestra
Set:	1026, 1028, 1029

Beswick		*Price*		
Number	*U.S. $*	*Can. $*	*U.K. £*	*Aust. $*
1027	75.00	100.00	25.00	75.00

1028
CAT WITH FIDDLE™

Designer:	Arthur Gredington
Height:	2", 5.0 cm
Colour:	Grey striped
Issued:	1945-1973
Series:	Cat Orchestra
Set:	1026, 1027, 1029

Beswick		*Price*		
Number	*U.S. $*	*Can. $*	*U.K. £*	*Aust. $*
1028	75.00	100.00	25.00	75.00

1029
CAT WITH SAXOPHONE™

Designer: Arthur Gredington
Height: 2", 5.0 cm
Colour: Grey striped
Issued: 1945-1973
Series: Cat Orchestra
Set: 1026, 1027, 1028

Beswick Number	*U.S. $*	*Price Can. $*	*U.K. £*	*Aust. $*
1029	75.00	100.00	25.00	75.00

1255
MONKEY WITH DRUM™

Designer: Jan Granoska
Height: 2 1/2", 6.4 cm
Colour: Brown and green
Issued: 1952-1963
Set: 1256, 1257, 1258, 1259, 1260

Beswick Number	*U.S. $*	*Price Can. $*	*U.K. £*	*Aust. $*
1255	200.00	275.00	125.00	200.00

1256
MONKEY WITH TUBA™

Designer: Jan Granoska
Height: 2 1/2", 6.4 cm
Colour: Brown and green
Issued: 1952-1963
Set: 1255, 1257, 1258, 1259, 1260

Beswick Number	*U.S. $*	*Price Can. $*	*U.K. £*	*Aust. $*
1256	200.00	275.00	125.00	200.00

1257
MONKEY WITH FIDDLE™

Designer: Jan Granoska
Height: 2 1/2", 6.4 cm
Colour: Brown and green
Issued: 1952-1963
Set: 1255, 1256, 1258, 1259, 1260

Beswick		*Price*		
Number	*U.S. $*	*Can. $*	*U.K. £*	*Aust. $*
1257	200.00	275.00	125.00	200.00

1258
MONKEY WITH SAXOPHONE™

Designer: Jan Granoska
Height: 2 1/2", 6.4 cm
Colour: Brown and green
Issued: 1952-1963
Set: 1255, 1256, 1257, 1259, 1260

Beswick		*Price*		
Number	*U.S. $*	*Can. $*	*U.K. £*	*Aust. $*
1258	200.00	275.00	125.00	200.00

1259
MONKEY WITH GUITAR™

Designer: Jan Granoska
Height: 2 1/2", 6.4 cm
Colour: Brown and green
Issued: 1952-1963
Set: 1255, 1256, 1257, 1258, 1260

Beswick		*Price*		
Number	*U.S. $*	*Can. $*	*U.K. £*	*Aust. $*
1259	200.00	275.00	125.00	200.00

1260
MONKEY WITH BANJO™

Designer: Jan Granoska
Height: 2 1/2", 6.4 cm
Colour: Brown and green
Issued: 1952-1963
Set: 1255, 1256, 1257, 1258, 1259

Beswick Number	*U.S. $*	*Price Can. $*	*U.K. £*	*Aust. $*
1260	200.00	275.00	125.00	200.00

INDICES

ALPHABETICAL INDEX OF FIGURINES

U

V

W

Y

Z

NUMERICAL INDEX TO BESWICK MODEL NUMBERS FOR ALICE IN WONDERLAND FIGURINES

NUMERICAL INDEX TO BESWICK MODEL NUMBERS FOR BEATRIX POTTER FIGURINES

2965	John Joiner
2966	Mother Ladybird
2971	Babbitty Bumble
2989	Tom Thumb
2996	Timmy Willie Sleeping
3006	Peter Rabbit Character Jug
3030	Tom Kitten and Butterfly
3031	Little Pig Robinson Spying
3088	Jemima Puddle-Duck Character Jug
3090	Mr. Jeremy Fisher Digging
3091	Mr. Tod
3094	Johnny Town-Mouse with Bag
3102	Mrs. Tiggy-Winkle Character Jug
3103	Tom Kitten Character Jug
3157	Peter Rabbit in the Gooseberry Net
3193	Jemima Puddle-Duck and Foxy Whiskered Gentleman
3197	Mittens and Moppet
3200	Gentleman Mouse Made a Bow
3219	Foxy Reading Country News
3220	Lady Mouse Made a Curtsey
3234	Benjamin Wakes Up
3242	Peter and the Red Pocket Handkerchief
3251	Miss Dormouse
3252	Pigling Eats His Porridge
3257	Christmas Stocking
3278	Mrs. Rabbit Cooking
3280	Ribby and the Patty Pan
3288	Hunca Munca Spills the Beads
3317	Benjamin Ate a Lettuce Leaf
3319	And This Pig Had None
3325	No More Twist
3473	Peter In Bed
3506	Mr. McGregor
3533	Peter Ate a Radish

NUMERICAL INDEX TO MODEL NUMBERS FOR BEATRIX POTTER STUDIO SCULPTURES FIGURINES

SS1	Timmy Willie
SS2	Flopsy Bunnies
SS3	Mr. Jeremy Fisher
SS4	Peter Rabbit
SS11	Mrs. Tiggy Winkle
SS26	Yock Yock (In the Tub)
SS27	Peter Rabbit (In the Watering Can)

NUMERICAL INDEX TO MODEL NUMBERS FOR BEDTIME CHORUS FIGURINES

1801	Pianist
1802	Piano
1803	Cat - Singing
1804	Boy Without Spectacles
1805	Boy With Spectacles
1824	Dog - Singing
1825	Boy With Guitar
1826	Girl With Harp

NUMERICAL INDEX TO MODEL NUMBERS FOR BESWICK BEARS FIGURINES

BB001	William
BB002	Billy
BB003	Harry
BB004	Bobby
BB005	James
BB006	Susie
BB007	Angela
BB008	Charlotte
BB009	Sam
BB010	Lizzy
BB011	Emily
BB012	Sarah

NUMERICAL INDEX TO DOULTON BRAMBLEY HEDGE FIGURINES

DBH1	Poppy Eyebright
DBH2	Mr. Apple
DBH3	Mrs. Apple
DBH4	Lord Woodhouse
DBH5	Lady Woodhouse
DBH6	Dusty Dogwood
DBH7	Wilfrid Toadflax
DBH8	Primrose Woodmouse
DBH9	Old Mrs. Eyebright
DBH10	Mr. Toadflax
DBH11	Mrs. Toadflax
DBH12	Catkin
DBH13	Old Vole
DBH14	Basil
DBH15	Mrs. Crustybread
DBH16	Clover
DBH17	Teasel
DBH18	Store Stump Money Box
DBH19	Lily Weaver
DBH20	Flax Weaver
DBH21	Conker
DBH22	Primrose Entertains
DBH23	Wilfrid Entertains
DBH24	Mr. Saltapple
DBH25	Mrs. Saltapple
DBH??	Dusty and Baby

NUMERICAL INDEX TO ROYAL DOULTON BUNNYKINS FIGURINES

D6001	Billy Bunnykins
D6002	Mary Bunnykins
D6003	Farmer Bunnykins
D6004	Mother Bunnykins
D6024	Freddie Bunnykins
D6025	Reggie Bunnykins
D6615A	Bunny Bank (First Version)
D6615B	Bunny Bank (Second Version)
DB1	Family Photograph Bunnykins (First Version)

DB123	Soccer Player Bunnykins
DB124	Rock'n'Roll Bunnykins
DB125	Milkman Bunnykins
DB126	Magician Bunnykins
DB127	Guardsman Bunnykins
DB128	Clown Bunnykins (First Version)
DB129	Clown Bunnykins (Second Version)
DB130	Sweetheart Bunnykins
DB131	Master Potter Bunnykins
DB132	Halloween Bunnykins
DB133	Aussie Surfer Bunnykins
DB134	John Bull Bunnykins
DB135	Constable Mountie Bunnykins
DB136	Sergeant Mountie Bunnykins
DB137	60th Anniversary Bunnykins
DB142	Cheerleader Bunnykins (First Version)
DB143	Cheerleader Bunnykins (Second Version)
DB144	Batsman Bunnykins
DB145	Bowler Bunnykins
DB146	Christmas Surprise Bunnykins
DB147	Rainy Day Bunnykins
DB148	Bathtime Bunnykins
DB149	Easter Greeting Bunnykins
DB150	Wicket Keeper Bunnykins
DB151	Partners in Collecting
DB152	Boy Skater Bunnykins
DB153	Girl Skater Bunnykins
DB155	Mother's Day Bunnykins
DB157	Goodnight Bunnykins
DB158	New Baby Bunnykins
DB160	Out For a Duck
DB161	Jester Bunnykins
DB6966A	City Gent Teapot
DB6966B	The Presidential Bunnykins Teapot

NUMERICAL INDEX TO MODEL NUMBERS FOR DAVID HAND'S ANIMALAND FIGURINES

1148	Dinkum Platypus
1150	Zimmy Lion
1151	Felia (Cat)
1152	Ginger Nutt
1153	Hazel Nutt
1154	Oscar Ostrich
1155	Dusty Mole
1156	Loopy Hare

NUMERICAL INDEX TO MODEL NUMBERS FOR ENGLISH COUNTRY FOLK FIGURINES

ECF1	Huntsman Fox
ECF2	Fisherman Otter
ECF3	Gardener Rabbit
ECF4	Gentleman Pig
ECF5	Shepherd Sheepdog
ECF6	Hiker Badger
ECF7	Mrs. Rabbit Baking
ECF8	The Lady Pig

NUMERICAL INDEX TO MODEL NUMBERS FOR JOAN WELSH ANGLUND FIGURINES

2272	Anglund Boy
2293	Anglund Girl with Doll
2317	Anglund Girl with Flowers

NUMERICAL INDEX TO MODEL NUMBERS FOR KITTY MCBRIDE FIGURINES

2526	A Family Mouse
2527	A Double Act
2528	The Racegoer
2529	A Good Read
2530	Lazy Bones
2531	A Snack
2532	Strained Relations
2533	Just Good Friends
2565	The Ring
2566	Guilty Sweethearts
2589	All I Do Is Think of You

NUMERICAL INDEX TO MODEL NUMBERS FOR LITTLE LIKABLES FIGURINES

LL1	Family Gathering (Hen and Two Chicks)
LL2	Watching the World Go By (Frog)
LL3	Hide and Seek (Pig and Two Piglets)
LL4	My Pony
LL5	On Top of the World (Elephant)
LL6	Treat Me Gently (Fawn)
LL7	Out of Last (Ducking)
LL8	Cats Chorus

NUMERICAL INDEX TO MODEL NUMBERS FOR LITTLE LOVABLES FIGURINES

LL1	Happy Birthday
LL2	I Love You
LL3	God Loves Me
LL4	Just For You
LL5	To Mother
LL6	Congratulations
LL7	Passed
LL8	Happy Birthday
LL9	I Love You
LL10	God Loves Me
LL11	Just For You
LL12	To Mother
LL13	Congratulations
LL14	Passed
LL15	Happy Birthday
LL16	I Love You
LL17	God Loves Me
LL18	Just For You
LL19	To Mother
LL20	Congratulations
LL21	Passed
LL29	To Daddy

LL30	Merry Christmas
LL31	Good Luck
LL32	Get Well Soon
LL33	Please
LL34	Please
LL35	I Love Beswick

NUMERICAL INDEX TO MODEL NUMBERS FOR THE PIG PROMENADE FIGURES

PP1	John the Conductor
PP2	Matthew the Trumpet Player
PP3	David the Flute Player
PP4	Andrew the Cymbal Player
PP5	Daniel the Violinist
PP6	Michael the Bass Drum Player
PP7	James The Triangle Player

NUMERICAL INDEX TO MODEL NUMBERS FOR RUPERT BEAR FIGURINES

2694	Rupert Bear
2710	Algy Pug
2711	Pong Ping
2720	Bill Badger
2779	Rupert Bear Snowballing

NUMERICAL INDEX TO ROYAL DOULTON SNOWMEN FIGURINES

DS1	James
DS2	The Snowman
DS3	Stylish Snowman
DS4	Thank You Snowman
DS5	Snowman Magic - Music Box
DS6	Cowboy Snowman
DS7	Highland Snowman
DS8	Lady Snowman
DS9	Bass Drummer Snowman
DS10	Flautist Snowman
DS11	Violinist Snowman
DS12	Pianist Snowman
DS13	Snowman's Piano
DS14	Cymbal Player Snowman
DS15	Drummer Snowman
DS16	Trumpeter Snowman
DS17	Cellist Snowman
DS18	Snowman Musical Box
DS19	Snowman Money Box
DS20	The Snowman Tobogganing
DS21	The Snowman Skiing
DS22	The Snowballing Snowman
DS23	Building the Snowman
D6972	Snowman Miniature Character Jug

NUMERICAL INDEX TO MODEL NUMBERS FOR THELWELL FIGURINES

2704A	An Angel on Horseback
2704B	An Angel on Horseback
2769A	Kick Start
2769B	Kick Start
2789A	Pony Express
2789B	Pony Express
SS7A	"I Forgive You"
SS7B	"I Forgive You"
SS12A	"Early Bath"
SS12B	"Early Bath"

NUMERICAL INDEX TO MODEL NUMBERS FOR THUNDERBIRDS FIGURINES

3337	Lady Penelope
3339	Brains
3344	Scott Tracy
3345	Virgil Tracy
3346	Parker
3348	The Hood

NUMERICAL INDEX TO MODEL NUMBERS FOR WALT DISNEY CHARACTERS FIGURINES

1278	Mickey Mouse
1279	Jiminy Cricket
1280	Pluto
1281	Goofy
1282	Pinocchio
1283	Donald Duck
1289	Minnie Mouse
1291	Thumper
1301	Nana
1302	Smee
1307	Peter Pan
1312	Tinkerbell
1325	Dopey
1326	Happy
1327	Bashful
1328	Sneezy
1329	Doc
1330	Grumpy
1331	Sleepy
1332A	Snow White (First Version)
1332B	Snow White (Second Version)
2193	Winnie the Pooh
2196	Eeyore
2214	Piglet
2215	Rabbit
2216	Owl
2217	Kanga
2394	Tigger
2395	Christopher Robin

NUMERICAL INDEX TO MODEL NUMBERS FOR WIND IN THE WILLOWS FIGURINES

2939	Mole
2940	Badger
2941	Ratty
2942	Toad
3065	Portly (Otter)
3076	Weasel Gamekeeper

NUMERICAL INDEX FOR MODEL NUMBERS FOR MISCELLANEOUS FIGURINES

1026	Cat Conductor
1027	Cat With Cello
1028	Cat With Fiddle
1029	Cat With Saxophone
1255	Monkey With Drum
1256	Monkey With Tube
1257	Monkey With Fiddle
1258	Monkey With Saxophone
1259	Monkey With Guitar
1260	Monkey With Banjo

Dear Royal Doulton and Beswick collector:

The Charlton Press has an ongoing commitment to excellence and thoroughness in all our Royal Doulton and Beswick reference books.

If you can help us by providing new or previously unobtainable data on any aspect of Doulton or Beswick figurines, we will consider including it in our subsequent editions. If accepted, your contribution will be acknowledged on the contributors' page at the front of the book.

We are seeking data on colourways, varieties, series, issue dates, designs and styles, as well as other information of interest to collectors. If you find any errors or omissions in our catalogues, please let us know. We particularly welcome photos of figurines that were marked "Photos not available at press time." Black-and-white, unscreened photographs are best.

Our 1996 schedule will include:

The Charlton Standard Catalogue of Beswick Animals - 2nd Edition
The Charlton Standard Catalogue of Royal Doulton Beswick Storybook Figurines - 3rd Edition
The Charlton Standard Catalogue of Royal Doulton Figurines - 5th Edition

Our 1997 schedule will include:

The Charlton Standard Catalogue of Royal Doulton Jugs - 4th Edition
The Charlton Standard Catalogue of Royal Doulton Beswick Storybook Figurines - 4th Edition
The Charlton Standard Catalogue of Royal Doulton Animals - 2nd Edition

Please send your information and photographs, together with your name, address and telephone number to:

Editorial Office
The Charlton Press
2010 Yonge Street
Toronto, Ontario
M4S 1Z9
Fax: (416) 488-4656